P9-CKN-282

Fashion Insiders' Guide
PARIS

Fashion Insiders' Guide

PARIS

Carole Sabas

Illustrated by Caroline Andrieu

Abrams | New York

Also Available: *Fashion Insiders' Guide—New York*

The material contained in this book is presented only for information and entertainment. The author and publisher have made every effort to present well-researched, accurate, reliable, and up-to-date information. However, the author and publisher cannot take any responsibility for any establishments that have closed since the publication of this work. Moreover, the publisher and author accept no responsibility or liability for any errors, omissions, or misrepresentations, expressed or implied, contained herein. The publisher and author have no financial interest in the businesses featured in this guide. The author is not a medical professional, and this information should not be considered medical advice. *This information should NOT be used to replace consultation with or treatment by a trained medical professional, therapist, or any other qualified expert.* The listing of a medical treatment or medical professional herein does not imply endorsement or recommendation by the author or publisher.

Editor: Deborah Aaronson
Designer: Christine Moog
Production Manager: Anet Sirna-Bruder

Cataloging-in-Publication Data has been applied for and may be obtained from the Library of Congress.
ISBN: 978-1-4197-0722-3

Printed and bound in China
10 9 8 7 6 5 4 3 2 1

Abrams books are available at special discounts when purchased in quantity for premiums and promotions as well as fundraising or educational use. Special editions can also be created to specification. For details, contact specialsales@abramsbooks.com or the address below.

THE ART OF BOOKS SINCE 1949

115 West 18th Street
New York, NY 10011
www.abramsbooks.com

CONTENTS

SHOPPING   134

MIGHT BE USEFUL ONE DAY   168

CREDITS & ACKNOWLEDGMENTS   187

"Yves Saint Laurent admired her and wanted to represent her. Half-loony, smoking in public places like Catherine Deneuve. Wearing fifteen-centimeter heels and her Chanel bag as if it were free. Wearing shouldered jackets because, indeed, everything starts with the shoulders. Eating crab in brasseries without fretting over staining her Céline blouse. Dropping everything if her heart says so."

—LOÏC PRIGENT
"The Parisian," French *Vogue*, August 2012

INTRODUCTION

Many times, I have been asked where to eat vegetables in Paris. Who is the best massage therapist to soothe jet lag? Where to get a serious blow-dry on short notice, a quick eyebrow shaping . . . ? I have too often failed to provide my sophisticated visiting friends with the right info. I have been living in NYC for five years now. For a long time, I wasn't aware of how different the routines and habits were between Paris and Manhattan. I could tell you where to buy cigarettes at 3:00 AM in Paris. But kale and scrambled tofu for breakfast? A myofascial release specialist? Hmm. Honestly, no idea. So I've decided to tackle that issue and give my New York, Milan, or São Paulo friends the best tips and favorite haunts from my people in Paris.

A quick caveat: This guide does not pretend to be authoritative. Sometimes the crowd in a restaurant will look more appealing than your food. And you may wonder why the tastemakers still come here season after season. Ask them and they'll shrug: "The owner is crazy."

Fashion people are creatures of habit. Not surprising, as their work is to program obsolescence. And they travel so much . . . the world, their playground. When it's time to relax, they look for their nests, wherever the photo shoot is taking place. Like a family, they also share the same strict code for a "stylish experience": fun characters, unpretentious luxe, impeccable professionalism, outsize punch, authenticity.

By following them, expect to be surprised, bewitched, puzzled, maybe disappointed at times, but always dazzled. That's what fashion is all about!

Have fun,

CAROLE SABAS

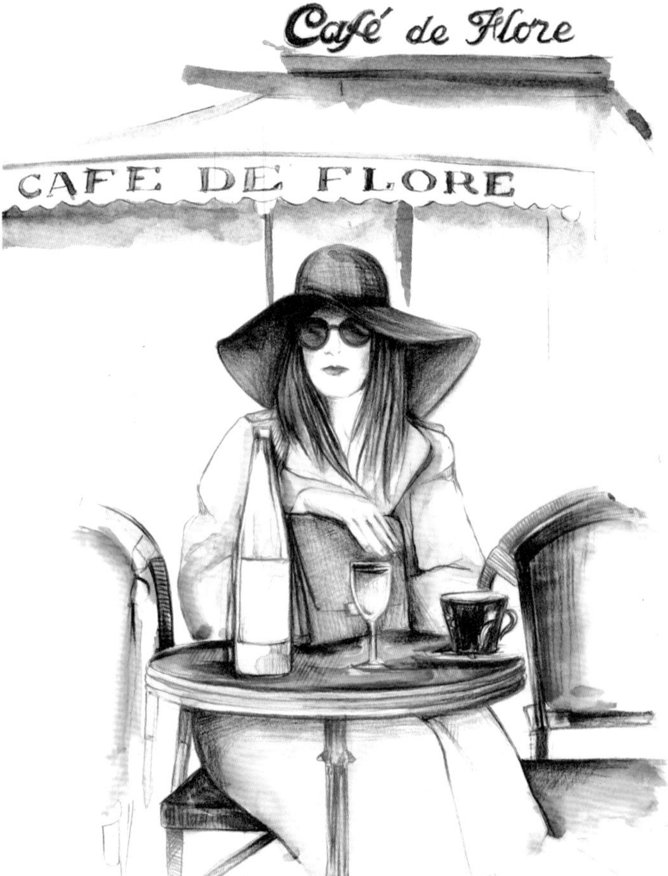
Café de Flore
CAFE DE FLORE

EATING, DRINKING & SLEEPING

VEGETARIAN RESTAURANTS

The healthy fashion-shoppers pick the *assiette colette* of steamed vegetables and mozzarella; the chicken, cucumber, and mint salad; or the cheesecake Mazaltov (fat-free) by Jean-Paul Hévin at COLETTE WATER BAR (213, rue Saint-Honoré, 75001; Tel. +33 1 55 35 33 90). Some go for the vegetarian entrées in fancy restaurants, like the curried tofu and the vegetable plates at the Karl Lagerfeld–approved LA SOCIÉTÉ (4, place Saint-Germain-des-Près, 75006; Tel. +33 1 53 63 60 60).

Until recently, steamed vegetables, perfectly al dente, were not exactly in the French culinary repertoire. At best, you could get your five daily servings from delicious stews, like the Arabic couscous or tagines that are still very popular. A new generation of young, cool restaurants, with sexy vegetable dishes that pummel your senses, has sprouted in Paris—a neo-rustic, botanical-chic trend that is now widely embraced. Below, some suggestions for lunches. For dinner, jump to "New Chic Chefs," p. 44.

Left Bank

For pure, hard-core, vegetarian places, emerging straight from the Flower Power era, go across La Seine. These places are also perfect for gluten-sensitive foodies.

GUEN MAÏ
6, rue Cardinale, 75006
Tel. +33 1 43 26 03 24

Battered and dusty enough to have served Marguerite Duras (who was a neighbor), this is a second-generation organic temple that caters to a (discreetly) star-studded crowd and New York It girls, such as Gaïa Repossi, with tofu ravioli and ginger-carrot juice. An adjacent store will refill your aromatherapy prescriptions—like the popular Fleur du Bach antistress vials. Lunch only.

TUGALIK
4, rue Toullier, 75005
Tel. +33 1 43 54 41 49

The restaurant is by the Pantheon, the sister fast-snack spot (29, rue Saint-Placide, 75006) is by the Bon Marché, but both offer healthy, fresh, exotic, nutritionist-approved creative cuisine (polenta tofu, lentils with coconut milk, gluten-free carrot cake). Only the restaurant is open for dinner.

LE GRENIER DE NOTRE-DAME
18, rue de la Bûcherie, 75005
Tel. +33 1 43 29 98 29

A very nonfancy, albeit stern, real-French-veggie experience in a medieval street of Paris's Rive Gauche. A cool, three-course menu at a bargain price.

Right Bank

BIOBOA

93, rue Montmartre, 75002
Tel. +33 1 40 28 02 83

This canteen is a 100 percent organic fresh-vegetable nirvana with non-vegetarian options. Its new, airy, spacious setting is the perfect stop for a wok of legumes and tofu or a delicious veggie burger, to be washed down with superfruit juice or, if you dare, a vodka-quinoa.

SOYA

20, rue de la Pierre-Levée, 75011
Tel. +33 1 48 06 33 02

Veggie and pretty and 100 percent organic, this rare restaurant was pointed out to us by Aurélie, from the diehard organic deli Le Retour à la Terre (leretouralaterre.fr). The location is a former faucet factory not far from the hip Canal Saint-Martin. Its communal tables are laden with from-all-over-the-world-inspired cuisine, from algae caviars to soy couscous. Plan B: ZUZU'S PETALS (8, rue Marie et Louise, 75010; Tel. +33 9 51 79 00 31).

VOY ALIMENTO

23, rue des Vinaigriers, 75010
Tel. +33 1 42 01 03 44

This microrestaurant is a wonderful concept, supported by none other than the great Alain Ducasse: a store and a cantina specializing in superfoods imported from Peru, Brazil, and Argentina loaded with powerful antioxidants, exotic flavors, and stunning ingredients with dreamy names—*klamath, ucurum* . . .

POUSSE POUSSE

7, rue Notre-Dame-de-Lorette, 75009
Tel. +33 1 53 16 10 81

A very chic deli and tiny cantina, the raw-food-culture embassy
in Paris, only open a few hours a week, also patronized by Alain
Ducasse. Test the classics, such as the perfect zucchini-tomato
spaghetti (gluten-free) or the cumin lentils. Plan B: M.O.B.
(30, rue Charlot, 75003; Tel. +33 1 42 77 51 05), a spin-off
of Maimonide of Brooklyn, from Mama Shelter's founders.

LE POTAGER DU MARAIS

22-24, rue Rambuteau, 75004
Tel. +33 1 57 40 98 57

A 99 percent organic institution, near Le Centre Georges Pompidou,
with creative cuisine inspired by French traditional fare, such as
seitan *bourguignon* and lasagnas.

ON THE FLY

On Rive Droite, the new healthy chains and glitzy "snackerias"
are trendy places for a quick bite.

COJEAN

17, boulevard Haussmann, 75009
3, place du Louvre, 75001
Other locations: cojean.fr

After ten years in Paris, COJEAN has grown into an impressive
chain, with more than fifteen locations all over town. Originally
in the Grands Boulevards area, opposite Le Figaro (it's also the
canteen inside the newspaper building), this sophisticated organic

"snackeria" offers decent juices and cool vegetarian plates, gyozas, noodle soups, veggie pies, and creative salads (lentils, orange) for a quick fix of healthy food.

QUALITÉ AND CO
7, rue du Marché Saint-Honoré, 75001
Tel. +33 1 44 50 00 04
37, rue de Berri, 75008
Tel. +33 1 40 74 00 74
4, rue de Choiseul, 75002
Tel. +33 1 40 15 09 99
Other locations: qualiteandco.com

These people are obsessed with natural and tasty antioxidants. Their cheap soups (creamy veggie with soy milk, carrot, honey, and cilantro . . .) are as delicious as their inventive juices.

SUM
49 bis, avenue Franklin D. Roosevelt, 75008
Tel. +33 1 53 76 32 83
13, rue des Pyramides, 75001
Tel. +33 1 40 15 62 91

A chic, self-service dim sum joint, the new craze in Paris, offering, whether to stay or to go, 100 percent natural, steamed, MSG-, oil-, and salt-free dishes in small bamboo baskets, prepared in front of you. Nonvegetarian (shrimp, chicken, beef) or 100 percent veggie options are available, both with rice cooked in a lotus leaf, to be washed down with a Pu-Erh tea.

JAPANESE RESTAURANTS

Rue Sainte-Anne and within a close radius is the epicenter of fashionable Japanese restaurants. From quick-bite cantinas to more sophisticated eateries, they are all democratic, gathering major stylists and power publicists alongside their assistants.

TAKARA
14, rue Molière, 75001
Tel. +33 1 42 96 08 38

A favorite of dandy designers Viktor & Rolf, TAKARA opened in 1958 and claims to be the oldest Japanese restaurant in Paris. Obviously it has never felt the impulse to revamp anything, from the waiters in kimonos to the vintage setting. Order the ultrafresh daikon-avocado salad, or browse the endless menu. And ask for table 14, in the quiet nook by the entrance.

KAÏ
18, rue du Louvre, 75001
Tel. +33 1 40 15 01 99

The bento-box lunch of this institution is fine, but we bet people-watching, or eavesdropping on the interview of a high-end designer or supermodel at the next table, will entertain you the most (this is a favorite place in Paris for this kind of exercise).

KUNITORAYA II
5, rue Villedo, 75001
Tel. +33 1 47 03 07 74

KUNITORAYA
39, rue Sainte Anne, 75001
Tel. +33 1 47 03 33 65

Udon (*nouilles*) is the specialty of this Japanese embassy of gourmet excellence, split into two nearby locations, one a formerly famous Parisian brasserie behind the Comédie Française. In both locations, the udon is the best in town, appreciated by all the most stylish experts on Japanese cuisine: Sarah from COLETTE calls KUNITO-RAYA II her cantine. And Sebastien Peigné—head of Mugler womenswear—always brings fashion superpower Nicola Formichetti —creative director at Mugler, Lady Gaga's stylist—to dine here.

TORAYA
10, rue Saint-Florentin, 75008
Tel. +33 1 42 60 13 00

Stepping into this fascinating *salon de thé* by the Place de la Concorde is like entering a Japanese air lounge of the seventies. We always imagine China Machado here, snacking on scrumptious pastries made of red beans with a perfect *matcha* tea. Lunch menus are sophisticated and pretty.

KINUGAWA

9, rue du Mont-Thabor, 75001
Tel. +33 1 42 60 65 07

A luxurious, authentic *kaiseki* cuisine specialist, KINUGAWA has been open for twenty years and is often crowded with high-fashion executives (Chanel headquarters are not far away). Praised by Gwyneth Paltrow, the restaurant serves impeccable sushi and sashimi, prepared to order right in front of you. Plus: The *Michelin Guide* roots for it.

YEN

22, rue Saint-Benoît, 75006
Tel. +33 1 45 44 11 18

Who comes here? Apparently everyone: Nathalie Rykiel, whose headquarters are nearby, the perfumer Frederic Malle, and the hot designer *du moment*, the Ministry of Culture-Andam-awarded Anthony Vaccarrello. This very upscale Japanese restaurant is chic, tasty, pricey, and minimal. It specializes in soba (buckwheat noodles), which are even better when served cold. The service is impeccable, the atmosphere rarefied—"perfect for business lunches."

TOYO

17, rue Jules-Chaplain, 76006
Tel. +33 1 43 54 28 03

Toyomitsu Nakayama, ex–private chef to Kenzo, splits his intricate cuisine between Japanese and French influences. From the open kitchen of this small Rive Gauche *gastronomique* restaurant, he focuses on stellar seafood and appeals essentially to a crowd of business people, gourmets, and Victoire de Castellane, the flamboyant grande dame of Dior jewelry.

GUILO GUILO

8, rue Garreau, 75018
Tel. +33 1 42 54 23 92

An exceptional Japanese experience, by Montmartre, including food and performance, both courtesy of the sexy, chic chef in white blouse and tie, Eiichi Edakuni. No menu, only the fresh specialties of the day, torqued to astound, such as foie gras sushi. Other key items: tofu with sea urchin and marinated catfish, eggplant and sea bream, candied pumpkin, etc. In your glass: bubble sake. Book weeks ahead.

Cheap and Quick

HIGUMA

32 bis, rue Sainte-Anne, 75001
Tel. +33 1 47 03 38 59
163, rue Saint-Honoré, 75001
Tel. +33 1 58 62 49 22

Many options on the menu, including gyozas, prepared in front of you, as well as ramen (broth with fresh noodles, pork, soybean sprouts). Long lines to get in, but quick service once inside.

LAÏ-LAÏ KEN

7, rue Saint-Anne, 75001
Tel. +33 1 40 15 96 90

This unassuming but consistent cantina is the regular haunt of many fashion editors despite its gloomy neon lighting. A mix of Chinese and Japanese. Scrumptious gyozas, soups, and *donburi* (mixed vegetable and rice bowls). Usually no wait.

AKI

11 bis, rue Sainte-Anne, 75001
Tel. +33 1 42 97 54 27

Serves the rare Osaka specialty *okonomiyaki* (an omelet with
cabbage and seafood or meat cooked on a hot plaque). Cool
wooden décor. Opposite is AKI BOULANGER (15, rue Sainte-Anne,
75001; Tel. +33 1 40 15 63 38) for desserts. Like a traditional
French bakery in décor, it offers surprising Japanese pastries,
such as *matcha*-melon *pan*, *yuzu* éclairs, green tea tiramisu,
and curry bread.

TAEKO

Marché des Enfants Rouge, 39, rue de Bretagne, 75003
Tel. +33 1 48 04 34 59

A wonderful, open-air Japanese canteen in the famous bobo
(*bourgeois boheme*) Marché des Enfants Rouge, this one far away
from rue Saint-Anne (it's in the Marais). Try the red-bean ice cream
if you're not full after your *donburi*. (NB: Isabel Marant always
points her visiting friends to this market: "So Parisian, simple and
friendly. A great mix of many cuisines, from Italian to Chinese
to Caribbean.")

Japanese Catering On Call

MAORI MUROTA

Contact: maorigohan@gmail.com

A self-taught freelance chef specializing in Japanese family cooking
"with lots of love," this former assistant to designer Christophe
Lemaire has many chic specialties, from *onigiri* to steamed
vegetables with tofu dip to crispy honey-and-black-pepper chicken.
She can prepare lunch boxes (bentos), like the ones she does at

lunchtime for LA CONSERVERIE (37 bis, rue du Sentier, 75002; Tel. +33 1 40 26 14 94), or she can cater special events as she has for Aesop and MERCI (see p. 138). Also vegetarian, vegan, and macrobiotic buffets.

LUNCH WITH GIRLFRIENDS

Lunchtime with a real friend always starts with: "See? No heels!" A promise that no fashion weapons will be used during that moment of truth and love.

NANASHI LE BENTÔ
31, rue de Paradis, 75010
Tel. +33 1 44 61 45 49
57, rue Charlot, 75003
Tel. +33 1 40 22 05 55

A great venue, courtesy of Lionel Bensemoun, the hipster entrepreneur from LE BARON (see p. 63). Bento boxes are filled with healthy, seasonal, organic superfoods (fish croquettes, salad, veggies, and quinoa) deliciously cooked by the former ROSE BAKERY (see p. 25) chef Kaori Endo. Try the perfect *chirashis* (mixed bowls). Two spin-offs of this Japanese-inspired canteen have opened: one in an airy location in the trendy northern Marais and another in the basement of the kids' fashion emporium BONPOINT (6, rue de Tournon, 75006; Tel. +33 1 43 26 14 06) on the Rive Gauche, with an endearing cobblestone terrace. Plan B: TARTES KLUGER (6, rue du Forez, 75003; Tel. +33 1 53 01 53 53). Right next door to the NANASHI LE BENTÔ MARAIS, the best for a creative "tart on the go" as fancy as carrot-lemon-coriander.

ROSE BAKERY

46, rue des Martyrs, 75009
Tel. +33 1 42 82 12 80
30, rue Debelleyme, 75003
Tel. +33 1 49 96 54 01
10, boulevard de la Bastille, 75012, inside the Art Foundation
La Maison Rouge
Tel. +33 1 46 28 21 14

Isabel Marant is particularly fond of these brunch/lunch gems: "very low profile, with retro atmosphere. I really enjoy going there, and I always get the same order: scrambled eggs with tomatoes and mushrooms, a green mint tea, brownies . . . The owner is an Englishwoman who also cooks organic vegetable tarts, salads, pancakes, and eggs. Everything is delicious, especially in the cakes department: shortbread, cookies, brownies, and a divine carrot cake. I have her cookbook, *Breakfast, Lunch and Tea*, and I love baking her cakes with my son."

BREAD AND ROSES

7, rue de Fleurus, 75006
Tel. +33 1 42 22 06 06
25, rue Boissy d'Anglas, 75008
Tel. +33 1 47 42 40 00

The quintessential bakery and deli-café with an obvious Anglo-Saxon twist, filled with ten-flour organic bread, pies, vegetable quiches, cheesecakes, salads, etc. (Caveat: Some disgruntled patrons have complained: "$$$$!") Catherine Deneuve, a neighbor, is said to love the one on the Left Bank, while the *Vogue* girls line up at the Right Bank location.

RIGHT BANK

BOB'S KITCHEN

74, rue des Gravilliers, 75003
Tel. +33 9 52 11 66

At the threshold of the Marais (at métro Arts & Métiers, not far from Jean Paul Gaultier's HQ), this is a very special English-speaking place where vegetarian breakfasts (incredibly good muffins) with American-standard juices start as early as 8:00 AM. Despite the tiny space, Marc Grossman does his best to get you a seat at lunchtime for a quick, scrumptious salad, soup, banana cream pie, or *futomaki*. A sister location, the JUICE BAR, in the trendy Canal Saint-Martin area, wakes up even earlier, at 7:30 AM (15, rue Lucien Sampaix, 75010; Tel. +33 9 50 06 36 18). BOB'S KITCHEN has also become a welcome spot for cool pop-up dinners, organized by The Sporting Project. It was here that France first met the hot New York boys of Manhattan's Fat Radish and Hudson Clearwater.

CUISSONS

65, rue de Saintonge, 75003
Tel. +33 1 44 78 96 92

Peter Karam, the former chef of Jean Paul Gaultier, can tell you cute stories of how his ex-boss used to require burgers of horse meat when he was sick (a homespun, grandmother's recipe). His canteen, white ceramic and reclaimed furniture, is the perfect stopover for a quick, healthy bite on your way to one of the Marais fashion showrooms or art galleries. Sexy vegetables, steamed al dente with lemon or ricotta, cod *brandade*, spinach pie with walnuts and scallions. Other options: MERCE AND THE MUSE (1 bis, rue Charles-François-Dupuis, 75003; Tel. +33 9 53 14 53 04): an

"American in Paris" that offers a festival of big salads, along with grilled vegetables and pies, in a comfy, trendy, and quaint street of the Carreau-du-Temple.

BREIZH CAFÉ
109, rue Vieille-du-Temple, 75003
Tel. +33 1 42 72 13 77

Cancale meets Tokyo in this popular crêperic, a love story between British and Japanese entrepreneurs and a hot spot of the upper Marais. Since 2007, it has welcomed all the stylish neighbors with organic buckwheat crêpes, ultrafresh oysters, and artisan ciders served by the Japanese staff. Next door, purchase the outstanding ingredients, from homemade jams to free-range eggs.

PATTAYA
29, rue Étienne-Marcel, 75001
Tel. +33 1 42 33 98 09

Why has this humble Thai restaurant become the lunch rendezvous of fashion people? Well, it's one block from Barbara Bui's fashion multistore Kabuki and a few steps from the Sentier—Paris's garment district. There is also the wry humor of the owner and the fine Asian cuisine with fair prices and consistent quality. Don't pay much attention to the décor. Be ready to say hi at least to one or two people.

LE FLORÉAL
73, rue du Faubourg-du-Temple, 75011
Tel. +33 1 40 18 46 79

Not far from Maison Margiela's HQ (and its press sales). Open all day long (8:00 AM–2:00 AM), this cool brasserie has saved the sixties' decoration of the old *bar-tabac* (red moleskin and Formica inside,

Mondrian geometry on the facade) but greatly improved the kitchen: cheeseburgers, seafood plates, and cocktails by the New Yorker David West. Alternatives by the Canal Saint-Martin (agnès b.'s HQ): Try LA CHAMBRE AUX OISEAUX (48, rue Bichat, 75010; Tel. +33 1 40 18 98 49). A big hit, from breakfast to lunch (or brunch), with its Greenpoint, Brooklyn, homey feeling. A hip sister of the beloved nearby brunch stronghold SESAME (151, quai de Valmy, 75010; Tel. +33 1 42 49 03 21), equally airy, with creative salads and house-baked desserts. Same area: Check out HELMUT NEWCAKE (36, rue Bichat, 75010; Tel. +33 9 82 59 00 39). A gluten-free bakery and *salon de thé,* with offerings from scrambled eggs and risottos to stellar wheat-free-flour tiramisu and *financiers.*

LEFT BANK

T'CHA
6, rue du Pont-de-Lodi, 75006
Tel. +33 1 43 29 61 31

An Asian restaurant and tea salon, very precious, a bit secluded, a
real girly girls' secret beloved by stylish French like Camille Miceli,
Dior's costume jewelry creative director. Just a few tables where
you can eat the perfectly perfumed fish of the day or tofu and black
sesame seeds. You'll also be introduced to the greatest teas, available
for purchase on the premises.

DEUX ABEILLES
189, rue Université, 75007
Tel. +33 1 45 55 64 04

The two busy bees are a mum and daughter who provide a cozy
and feminine atmosphere for a feel-good lunch or teatime by the
Pont de l'Alma. Emmanuelle Alt, the editor of French *Vogue*, purrs
over their tomato pies and homemade sodas.

RALPH'S RESTAURANT
173, boulevard Saint-Germain, 75006
Tel. +33 1 44 77 76 00

Set in a seventeenth-century mansion, Ralph Lauren's in-store
restaurant has become the favorite spot for jet-setters for a nice
catch up between business trips. Laure Heriard Dubreuil, owner of
Miami fashion store The Webster, raves about the hamburgers, the
Cobb salad ("a rarity in Paris"), and the carrot cake. ("Love
the complimentary caramel popcorn with coffee, too!")

BAR DE LA CROIX ROUGE

2, carrefour de la Croix-Rouge, 75006
Tel. +33 1 45 48 06 45

A staple for Parisian stylists and designers, who love to meet here to share a glass of Brouilly and one of the delicious *tartine au pain Poilâne* with thin slices of roast beef, tomatoes, pickles, and creamy mustard on greens.

STYLISH ITALIAN

Professional lunches with a fashion publicist in Paris often take place in one of these legendary trattorias. On the map because of the neighborhood (where the major houses cluster), their high standard of service, their fresh antipasti, and something in the atmosphere that immediately eases the meetings from "vous" to "tu."

LE STRESA

7, rue Chambiges, 75008
Tel. +33 1 47 23 51 62

A stalwart, because of its location in the Triangle d'Or (the crossroads of high-end fashion in Paris). LA STRESA has been managed by the same family for decades. Among the well-groomed executives of the couture houses, you can imagine the French hero Jean-Paul Belmondo indulging in risotto *aux girolles* or the pasta named after him, a signature dish and house homage.

CASA BINI

36, rue Grégoire-de-Tours, 75006
Tel. +33 1 46 34 05 60

Nothing special in the vintage décor, but fresh products and constant elegance entwined with reasonable prices. This explains why this

quiet Toscane trattoria is still on the high-powered publicists'
Rolodex. An outpost of CASA BINI has opened at PRIMO PIANO,
the gracefully designed and shaded terrace on the second floor of the
department store LE BON MARCHÉ RIVE GAUCHE (see p. 136).

CIBUS
5, rue Molière, 75001
Tel. +33 1 42 61 50 19

A pure Sicilian at heart, so tiny that only three or four tables
(sixteen seats exactly) fit inside, but spectacular enough to impress
an Italian connoisseur like the communications director of
Diesel. The restaurant welcomes the guest VIPs of neighbor *Purple
Magazine*, the likes of Marc Jacobs, and It girls from Anja Rubik
to Caroline de Maigret. The owner will decide what you eat. And
you'll happily comply.

LE CHERCHE MIDI
22, rue du Cherche-Midi, 75006
Tel. +33 1 45 48 27 44

A landmark since 1978, where famous actors and neighbors alike
mingle graciously with a crowd of well-heeled locals (the jeweler
Aurélie Bidermann calls the place "my HQ") and romantic diners.
A nice pause in the middle of a shopping binge on the rue de
Grenelle, even if we've lately heard complaints of a slight downslide
in quality. Plus: Open seven days a week.

FULVIO
4, rue de Poitou, 75003
Tel. +33 1 42 71 62 80

A Sardinian nest for the avant-garde publicists and trendy designers
like Anthony Vaccarello, who say (with all due respect and affection):
"The owner is crazy and insists on explaining his menu and his

burrata—a 'why it's the best' kind of explanation—to each table."
Expect more to-die-for al dente pastas (truffle sauce orrechiete,
linguini and red mullet . . .) than light antipasti.

LA FARNESINA
9, rue Boissy-d'Anglas, 75008
Tel. +33 1 42 66 65 57

A sophisticated cantina, with its dramatic paintings al fresco and its
perfect grilled vegetables *à la plancha*. By the Place de la Concorde,
a common hangout for the staff of *Vogue* at lunchtime.

LES VITELLONI
4, rue Dupetit-Thouars, 75003
Tel. +33 1 48 87 38 45

In the romantic and peaceful Carreau du Temple area, a stone's
throw from the OFR BOOKSTORE (see p. 176) and *Libération*
newspaper, it's the quintessential fashion spot, with a terrace full of
in-the-know models (Anja Rubik) and designers (Kriss Van Assche).
Daily menu, grilled vegetables, mad tiramisu, and exceptional
olive oil.

EMPORIO ARMANI CAFFÈ
149, boulevard Saint-Germain, 75006
Tel. +33 1 45 48 62 15

Was all the rage when it opened in 2010, with its strategic terrace,
the ideal cast of professional and smiling staff, and the perfectly
chic burrata, roquette, and tomato salad.

ENZA & FAMIGLIA
89, rue Saint-Honoré, 75001
Tel. +33 1 40 41 06 25

Two sisters' microcanteen for classic Italian fare: bruschetta, polenta, and perfectly cooked fettuccine subtly highlighted with a light zip of olive and truffle oils. Currently, the best Italian catering for big fashion houses. We have promised: no names. But their references are impressive enough for you to order that special-event buffet right away.

EARLY BREAKFAST OR LAZY TEATIME

CLAUS
14, rue Jean-Jacques Rousseau, 75001
Tel. +33 1 42 33 55 10
Scones, homemade muesli, and cookies, anyone? This small German candy-box-like café/épicerie was opened across from Louboutin, near passage Véro-Dodat, by a former fashion publicist (YSL, Givenchy). Starts serving at 7:30 AM his ideal *frühstück*: perfect scrambled eggs, homemade yogurts, and cornflakes. The tables upstairs—retro-pop-chic décor—also cater to your midafternoon sweet craving or need for a quick lunch (sautéed *girolles*). Try the nectars by Alain Milliat or the herbal teas of HERBORISTERIE DU PALAIS ROYAL (see p. 54).

LADURÉE
75, avenue des Champs-Élysées, 75008
Tel. +33 1 40 75 08 75
16, rue Royale, 75008
Tel : +33 1 42 60 21 79
Other locations: laduree.fr
Since opening on Madison Avenue in 2011, this *macaron* institution has sparked an international trend about to knock down the *Sex and the City*–era cupcake. Stop by the original location on rue Royal, with its quaint Napoleon III candy-box décor, at 8:00 AM,

when it's already filled with Hermès and L'Oréal executives having early meetings.

CARETTE
4, place du Trocadéro, 75016
Tel. +33 1 47 27 98 85
25, place des Vosges, 75003
Tel. +33 1 48 87 94 07

If you're ready to indulge, CARETTE is the place, since 1927. An emblem of conservative chic, not far from the Eiffel Tower. The fashion stylists love to stop by before a show at the Musée de L'Homme for a quick salad or house ice cream. There is now a trendier version under the historic arcades of the place des Vosges, with décor by Hubert de Givenchy (the nephew), touristy and sweetly decadent. Both locations offer good breakfast options and open early (7:00 AM at Trocadéro, 8:00 AM at Place des Vosges).

LE TÉLESCOPE
5, rue Villedo, 75001
Tel. +33 1 42 61 33 14

A rare, tiny, Brooklyn-style option in Paris for coffee snobs: the beans come from Colombia or Kenya and are home-roasted and drip-filtered through a state-of-the-art La Marzocco machine. Complement your coffee with baked goods, granola, and jams. A stylish spot for an early-morning interview with the neighboring journalists of the historic weekly *Nouvel Observateur* and *Obsession* (its style supplement).

BRUNCH

CENTRE D'ART-CAFÉ LE BAL

6, impasse de la Défense, 75018

Tel. +33 1 44 70 75 51

Hidden behind the gritty Place de Clichy, LE BAL combines an exhibition space dedicated to photography and a bookstore with a pleasant and light-filled deli/café. It serves great British plates (the chefs are alumnae of ROSE BAKERY, see p. 25) and smart wines in an unexpectedly quaint, no-cars-allowed cobblestone street. Remote and all the rage among the Vélib' bike sharers. Play it as it lays, and go for the most exotic (meat stews) or the classics (scones, eggs). Check out the bookstore and the photo exhibition space downstairs, linked to the legendary photo agency Magnum.

LE MARCEL
1, villa Léandre, 75018
Tel. +33 1 46 06 04 04

Another British-inspired address in the lovely, leafy, wealthy part of Montmartre, one step from the quaint HÔTEL PARTICULIER (see p. 75). Fish and chips, pancakes, and cheesecake appeal to the stylish throngs who flock here for the all-day weekend brunch. The poster child of the Paris *bobo* haunts.

L'AMOUR
8, rue Navarin, 75009
Tel. +33 1 48 78 31 80

The restaurant seams to target (respect?) only the cool hipsters (ex: "Hey, isn't that Andrea Casiraghi on the terrace?"). But with its fresh-ingredients cuisine and its green outdoor patio, it has become a coveted spot, especially for post-hangover weekend brunches. Pancakes, Champagne, and bread from the famous local Delmontel bakery.

OLDIES BUT GOODIES

How to dine amid the fashion glitterati? Where to lunch with a head buyer or influential journalist? You'll never make a fashion faux pas with these landmarks. Be aware of the Fashion Week dates, though, as it might be impossible even to get close to these prestigious banquettes (2013: Sept. 24–Oct. 2; 2014: Feb. 25–Mar. 5, Sept. 23–Oct. 1).

CAVIAR KASPIA
17, place de la Madeleine, 75008
Tel. +33 1 42 65 33 32

Glowing and epicentral, especially during Fashion Weeks. Opened in 1927, it was once the favorite joint of aristocratic Russian expats and Ballets Russes *mécènes*. Cheeky, it's now surfing on the *air du temps*, collaborating with the likes of impresario André, who signed a limited-edition caviar box in 2012, but it has remained the almighty place to have fun while doing business in Paris. The forever favorite of the fashion bold-faced, especially when on expense accounts.

LE VOLTAIRE
27, quai Voltaire, 75007
Tel. +33 1 42 61 17 49

Well-heeled locals and A-class fashion designers, plus occasional American celebrities (Charlize Theron and Cindy Sherman have been spotted here), absolutely love this elegant, classic bistro by the Seine, in the same building where the eighteenth-century writer and philosopher passed away. It still kind of holds its own, despite the aloof service, thanks to its history and its traditional, well-executed cuisine.

MAISON PRUNIER
16, avenue Victor-Hugo, 75016
Tel. +33 1 44 17 35 85

CAFÉ PRUNIER
15 place de la Madeleine, 75008
Tel. +33 1 47 42 98 91

A real French haute-gastronomy experience, courtesy of the owner, Pierre Bergé, YSL's legendary partner and guru of the political and cultural life in Paris for more than fifty years. Both locations are favored by young fashion star Guillaume Henry (the Carven designer whom Net-à-porter's founder called a "young YSL") and his ilk. Henry loves the Jacques Grange (Madeleine) or genuine 1920s (Victor Hugo) lavish décor equally, their seafood specialty (smoked salmon and the famous low-salt French caviar), and desserts carousel. Sterling service, too.

LE DUC
243, boulevard Raspail, 75014
Tel. +33 1 43 20 96 30

Another Paris staple, in the business of über-fresh seafood for a few decades (President Mitterrand was a regular). A recent celebrity seen here was Balenciaga perfume spokesperson Kristen Stewart. But the discreet place attracts many VIPs with its signature salmon tartare, which seems even more enjoyable in the nautical setting.

L'ASTRANCE
4, rue Beethoven, 75016
Tel. +33 1 40 50 84 40

A favorite of aesthete Nathalie Rykiel, the Astrance provides a real foodie experience with a menu-free policy, which means that you have to surrender yourself to the chef—a possibly life-changing experience for control-freak fashion-studio managers.

THIOU
49, quai d'Orsay, 75007
Tel. +33 1 40 62 96 50

Regularly mentioned as one of the ten best restaurants in Paris, this deluxe Thai eatery welcomes many successful, creative, and blue-chip patrons, from magazine honchos to world-class stylists to Marc Jacobs (a regular, swear our friends). Bonus: Open every day, all year long. Plan B: For Thai food behind the romantic Palais Royal Gardens: BAAN BORAN (43, rue de Montpensier, 75001; Tel. +33 1 40 15 90 45).

LA CIGALE RÉCAMIER
4, rue Récamier 75007
Tel. +33 1 45 48 86 58

A favorite of jewelers, those of Place Vendôme or independent talents like Aurélie Bidermann. The specialty of the restaurant is the soufflé in all its possible variations. It is available here salted or sweet, from appetizer to entrée to dessert. And don't worry about getting bored: The menu is seasonal.

DAVÉ
12, rue de Richelieu, 75001
Tel. +33 1 42 61 49 48

We recommend that anyone tempted to follow the American editors here first read the 2004 *New Yorker* article about this Chinese high-fashion cafeteria, exposing the startling rules of seating arrangements. What you want is the front room. But Davé himself will let you know where you rank. Less influential nowadays (the food quality, maybe?) but still on the map.

MINI PALAIS
3, avenue Winston Churchill, 75008
Tel. +33 1 42 56 42 42

Practically on the path of the Chanel runway, twice a year set in the grandiose building of the Grand Palais. Not an oldie (it opened in fall 2010) but a goodie, for sure. The consultant chef, Eric Fréchon (from the Bristol), boasts three Michelin stars. Pointed out to us by Thomas Persson, the editor in chief of *Acne Paper*: "My favorite spot in Paris, on its terrace, beneath the arcades." Bonus: Open until 2:00 AM.

RESTAURANT DU PALAIS ROYAL
110, galerie de Valois, 75001
Tel. +33 1 40 20 00 27

One of the most gorgeous and romantic terraces (open from April to September) in the dreamland of the Palais Royal, gardens, and arcades. Best part is the adjacent, bi-level Rick Owens store, which carries all his clothing collections, plus his cultural *coups de coeurs* (DVDs of *Boom!*, *Olympia*, and *Der Ring des Niebelungen*, or the book *Down the Garden Path* [1932] by Beverley Nichols, a snobby and funny British gardening writer). Good to know, fans, if you can't exactly afford that 2,000€, butter-soft leather jacket.

BISTRONOMY

A bistro for real gourmets, visiting supermodels, and fashion designers is called a "bistronomy," a makeover that started in the early 2000s. Bistronomy refuses to conform to bistro stereotypes but still celebrates them.

LE CHATEAUBRIAND
129, avenue Parmentier, 75011
Tel. +33 1 47 63 96 90

This one is old news but still at the top of the list for world-famous fashion people, plus David Chang of Momofuku. All are fans of Iñaki Aizpitarte, the superstar chef who also does wonders at LE DAUPHIN (see p. 44). Major stylists rave about the foie gras–strawberry sauce. Plan B: ANAHI (49, rue Volta, 75003; Tel. +33 1 48 87 88 24), an Argentinian meat mecca since the nineties, with the same hard-chairs-bare-tables-for-real-foodies vibe.

FERDI

32, rue du Mont-Thabord, 75001

Tel. +33 1 42 60 82 52

An international crossroads for stylists, fashion photographers, and designers since the cult buyer Maria Luisa initiated the birth of the restaurant by her former store. Everybody enjoys the house Bloody Mary, risotto, and ceviche, as well as the Latin vibe and the mandatory "Hey! Good to see you!" that comes with Fashion Weeks. The cheeseburgers are the best in Paris, Penelope Cruz may have said. Plan B: Burger lovers should follow Lou Douillon and Diane Kruger to COFFEE PARISIEN (4, rue Princesse, 75006; Tel. +33 1 43 54 18 18).

LA FIDÉLITÉ

12, rue de la Fidélité, 75010

Tel. +33 1 47 70 19 34

Rock ironic, retro chic with its art deco ceilings, basic menu, and outstanding wines, La Fidélité has been meta-cool since André and Lionel (LE BARON; p. 63) worked their magic. Dress code is skinny jeans and serious arm candy. Cigarettes and preclubbing downstairs. Private room upstairs.

AU PASSAGE

1 bis, passage Saint-Sébastien, 75011

Tel. +33 1 43 55 07 52

The 2012 favorite of the gourmet photographer The Selby, this vintage café-restaurant is hidden not far from the *bobo* bazaar MERCI (see p. 138). It is hip again since being taken over by a team of dynamic young entrepreneurs who worked at upgrading duck breast, veal liver, and monkfish. Budget pleasing and open late, with great-quality wines.

MIROIR

94, rue des Martyrs, 75018

Tel. +33 1 46 06 50 73

Beloved by foreign visitors for its caring waiters who can translate into English the chalkboard full of ultrafresh products and fashionable vintage vegetables. Plus, the local vibe is intense. Perfect for an initiation into truly French experiences such as veal tongue and *andouillette*, served amid Isabel Marant–clad neighbors and the cool electronic-music crowd from Les Abbesses.

PÉTRELLE

34, rue Pétrelle, 75009

Tel. +33 1 42 82 11 02

We used to see the cream of the crop of creative jet-setters like Marie-Hélène de Taillac in this whimsical boudoir, which looks more like a cabinet of curiosities signed by Helena Cristensen, than a quality restaurant. Come here to test the *Gault&Millau*-recommended scampi with asparagus, grilled sweetbreads, and some of the heirloom vegetables served daily by the creative chef. Finish with a lavender-flavored crème. Have a look at the Tumblr-like website (petrelle.fr) as a warm-up.

CHEZ MOUSTACHE

4, rue Jean-Pierre Timbaud, 75011

Tel. +33 1 43 38 26 88

A tip from Mikael Schiller, glam boss of Acne Studios: "The year we opened a new store at rue Froissat, an old Parisian friend took me to a new restaurant in the same area, CHEZ MOUSTACHE. The food was great, the crowd interesting . . . ," and the rest is history. Since then nicknamed the "gentlemen's lair" by the French media.

NEW CHIC CHEFS

Sporting tattoos, black tees, and blue aprons, the new chefs are electrifying Paris with cuisine as creative, modern, whimsical, and seasonal as that found in Williamsburg. Actually, the ultimate compliment for a French chef right now is "So Brooklyn!" For health maniacs, many new options in the gastronomic range.

LE DAUPHIN
131, avenue Parmentier, 75011
Tel. +33 1 55 28 78 88
Rem Koolhaas, Muccia Prada's best friend, designed this marble box, an offspring of next-door LE CHATEAUBRIAND (p. 41), with a U-shaped counter. Iñaki Aizpitarte, the trailblazer of the sexy-young-chefs trend in Paris, and his cool staff serve a bunch of delicious tapas, or *rationes*, salty or sweet, perfect for portion-controlled diets.

VIVANT ·
43, rue des Petites Ecuries, 75010
Tel. +33 1 42 46 43 55
"Pierre Jancou is that tattooed quadra whom all the girls fancy," introduces one of our friends. Everybody loves his "neo" bistro set in a former bird shop, with splendid, painted earthenware walls from 1903 and fifties Formica furniture. Come here for the seasonal menus, and exceptional products used to create natural, simple ("*sans chichi*," in French, "no nonsense" in English), essentially rustic fare (Challans duck or line-caught pollack) and organic wines.

SEPTIME

80, rue de Charonne, 75011

Tel. +33 1 43 67 38 29

The A.P.C. and Armani patrons love it. Scandinavian-style décor and heavy gravy–free cuisine by a gifted maniac of fresh products, Bertrand Grébaut, a thirty-something former graphic designer who started all over with Alain Passard, the maestro who spearheaded the French vegetable renaissance. Plan B: Grab the best organic local fruits at the equally chic next-door MAISON POS (90, rue de Charonne, 75011; Tel. +33 1 43 70 83 01).

FRENCHIE

5, rue du Nil, 75002

Tel. +33 1 40 39 96 19

With its reputation for coolness, this new spot, a loft look-alike, offers a new twist on traditional French cuisine, now light and exciting, where vegetables are, indeed, fully part of the experience. Sublime international wines, here and across the street, at the small bar open for cognoscenti (6, rue de Nil). Dinner only.

SPRING

6, rue Bailleul, 75001

Tel. +33 1 45 96 05 72

Expect a few months on a waiting list; it's the rule of this discreet restaurant-*buvette* with dark wood furniture, stern atmosphere, and an already-prestigious reputation among fashion gourmets (Sarah from COLETTE . . .). Fresh products are the only constant of the menu, which changes daily, upon the (American) chef's inspiration. With an "on the go" outpost nearby (52, rue de l'Arbre-Sec, 75001).

YAM'TCHA
4, rue Sauval, 75001
Tel. +33 1 40 26 08 07

Jean-Charles de Castelbajac—whose studio is nearby—is loyal to this cantina deluxe, actually one of the most distinguished Asian-fusion tables in Paris. Reservations are mandatory and hard to get, but the experience is unique and worth the fight. Dinner with nine courses, including lobster with corn coulis and poached egg yolk, has never tasted so good with an Oolong tea.

LA DAME DE PIC
20, rue du Louvre, 75001
Tel. +33 1 42 60 40 40

A sensation at its inception in fall 2012, this gourmet restaurant is the brainchild of Anne-Sophie Pic, world's best female chef of 2011. Her meals—three courses and a dessert—are built like a perfume, around a main note ("amber vanilla," "iodine and flowers" . . .), with ultrafresh products, organic vegetables, and sophisticated broths.

OLD-TIMERS AND BRASSERIES

Originally open 24/7, these are the places for an initiation into Continental, preindustrial comfort food amid genuine décor. Stuffed veal chest, cheek of beef, tartare (raw beef) *au couteau*, steak with gravy *béarnaise*, charcuterie, leeks drowned in vinaigrette, herring and potato salad, crème caramel, etc.—the French version of comfort foods is barely translatable and strictly nonexportable.

LE COMPTOIR DU RELAIS
9, carrefour de l'Odéon, 75006
Tel. +33 1 44 27 07 97

In fashion land, things are not what they used to be, cool-wise, so here we are, in this old-school brasserie, surrounded by the most revered young faces of the industry in Paris, Capucine Safyurtlu from *Vogue* and Anthony Vaccarello, who names it "my favorite place in Paris to celebrate, post-show, with my friends."

CHEZ RENÉ
14, boulevard Saint-Germain, 75005
Tel. +33 1 43 54 30 23

The smart fashion publicists take their American editors to efficient press lunches in this typical Lyon brasserie. It is tourist-free and so quaint that it would be the perfect setting for a key scene in a sequel to *Midnight in Paris*. Order meat and French fries or that ancestral, staid stew called *boeuf bourguignon*.

BALZAR
49, rue des Écoles, 75005
Tel. +33 1 43 54 13 67

Appealing to Sorbonne scholars, political-science teachers, and the fashion set (such as Mugler womenswear designer Sebastien Peigné and his creative director, Nicola Formichetti), this place is a legend. So much so that a *New Yorker* correspondent covered in an extensive story its takeover by an industrial group in 1998 and the uproar among its patrons that ensued. Leather banquettes, globe lamps, white linens, sparkling silver . . . More than a decade later, everything is settled and Balzar is back to its legendary looks.

BRASSERIE LIPP

151, boulevard Saint-Germain, 75005

Tel. +33 1 45 48 53 91

The quintessence of nineteenth-century Alsacian brasseries—indestructible, arrogant, powerful, with an intricate seating protocol hostile to nobodies and tourists—Lipp could be to Paris what Michael's or the Four Seasons is to New York: a daily Pazz & Jop of the media, publishers, and politicians in town. At night, some fashion bold-face names sit downstairs, appeasing their craving for a cassoulet.

BENOÎT

20, rue Saint-Martin, 75004

Tel. +33 1 42 72 25 76

Michelin-approved, Alain Ducasse–managed, this brasserie is a political haunt but can also appeal to visiting fashion queens (Nathalie Massenet, founder of Net-à-porter, and Claudia Schiffer have lunched together here). It will introduce you to the joys of *paté en croûte* and *tête de veau sauce ravigote*. Open on Sundays.

MOM AND POP DINERS

You might not believe that the fashion intelligentsia love these places, but they do, prizing soul and authenticity. The worst sin in French fashion is being *chichiteux* (prissy). These joints are anything but, and that's what our no-nonsense trailblazers seek.

LA LAITERIE SAINTE CLOTILDE

64, rue de Bellechasse, 75007

Tel. +33 1 45 51 74 61

A little candlelit flea market with 1970s-style furnishings, this

neighborhood joint is all about traditional comfort food (we're reluctant to translate *blanquette de veau*). Recently on the fashion radar, God or Gucci knows why.

LE HANGAR
12, impasse Berthaud, 75003
Tel. +33 1 42 74 55 44
A longtime favorite of fashion talents like the "sophisti-pop accessories" creator Yazbukey. A neighbor, she can often be found in the back of this regional-dishes restaurant. Her mascot, Viktor, is usually asleep in his Z Spoke dog carrier. Nothing stylish in this tucked-away establishment except what's on your plate: perfect samples of well-prepared French cuisine, alongside impeccable wines.

CHEZ LA VIEILLE ADRIENNE

1, rue Bailleul, 75001

Tel. +33 1 42 60 15 78

Only five tables, and you will need to call ahead to score one. Buzz "Adrienne" at this very special address of old Paris, a historic bistro with a private salon on the second floor and a fine vernacular cuisine including *navarin de veau* (veal stew), *daurade au vin blanc* (sea bream in white wine), and chocolate pie.

CHEZ FRANÇOISE

Esplanade des Invalides, under the Air France Aérogare, underground level, 75007

Tel. +33 1 47 05 49 03

A traditional, immaculate-white-tablecloth, bourgeois restaurant, which has tourists and locals raving. Even more interesting than the appetizers of layers of eggplant are the special Saturday *soirées musicales et gastronomiques* . . . at least when they welcome the iconoclast American artist Christeene to perform his hits ("Tears from My Pussy". . .) as specially invited by Rick Owens and Michele Lamy, two regulars.

RED-AND-WHITE-CHECKED NAPKINS

Another roundup of genuine fashion haunts, which might only appeal to those craving the perennial Parisian traditions: comfort food and brisk service.

CHEZ GEORGES

1, rue du Mail, 75002
Tel. +33 1 42 60 07 11

Years ago, when Alber Elbaz was setting up a lunch interview "chez George," you would head to the sleek, modern-chic restaurant at Centre George Pompidou without giving it a second thought. Wrong. He wanted you here, at this prewar kitchen, where you can taste incredible vernacular foodstuffs, including veal liver and beef kidneys. End the experience with a full bowl of raspberries and cream, served by old ladies in traditional aprons.

CHEZ DENISE

La Tour de Montlhéry, 5, rue des Prouvaires, 75001
Tel: +33 1 42 36 21 82

A legendary bistro of the Halles, when the area was called the Hole (it is again, as the disastrous 1980s mall buildings have just been razed for 2014 construction). It looks its age (thirty years), but it is open day and night, perfect if you are craving house foie gras, escargots, marrow bones, or terrific steak frites (fries) at 4:00 AM, in a communal atmosphere.

BAR À VINS LE RUBIS

10, rue du Marché Saint-Honoré, 75001
Tel. +33 1 42 61 03 34

A small fiftieslike hot spot, where Juliette Greco and Michèle Bernstein, muses of the Situationists, could have swilled red wine and puffed Gauloises at the counter, while poets in black turtlenecks vamped. Lunch consists of greasy plates of cheese and charcuterie, lentil salads, and apricot pies. Downright antifashion but totally Parisian—a tip from Sarah (of COLETTE).

SHOPPING GOURMET

Feeling more adventurous than Dalloyau, Fauchon, Hédiard, Lenôtre, La Grande Epicerie De Paris, Jean-Paul Hévin, Pierre Hermé, or Maison du Chocolat? Here some insiders' backups.

FROMAGERIE NICOLE BARTHÉLÉMY

51, rue de Grenelle, 75007
Tel. +33 1 45 48 56 75

Here you can experience the smelliest French cheeses in a very quaint setting. The owner selects the best ones and keeps them in his basement until they reach perfection, and many fashion customers then pick up their Mont d'Or.

DU PAIN ET DES IDÉES

34, rue Yves Toudic, 75010
Tel. +33 1 42 40 44 52

In its nineteenth-century premises, this bakery holds sway among the new generation of fashion cognoscenti, who line up for its rustic breads. On the Left Bank, the older French editors send their assistants to get their sandwiches at GÉRARD MULOT, another upper-crust bakery, with locations on both banks (6, rue du Pas-de-la-Mule, 75003; Tel. +33 1 42 78 52 17 and 76, rue de Seine, 75006; Tel. +33 1 43 26 85 77).

JOËL THIEBAULT

Marché du Président Wilson, avenue du Président Wilson, 75016
Every Wednesday and Saturday morning, this revered farmer caters to the vegetable lovers and grands chefs of Paris with his four-meter-long table of heirloom veggie varieties locally produced in his fields. Also available online at lehautdupanier.com and tousprimeurs.com.

WORKSHOP ISSÉ
11, rue Saint-Augustin, 75002
Tel. +33 1 42 96 26 74

A favorite of all the diehard fans of and experts in Japanese culture in Paris. They appreciate and willingly promote this fine épicerie, provider of the best *tosazu* vinegars, *yuzu* juices, and gourmet sakes.

LA CAVE DU DARON
140, avenue Parmentier, 75011
Tel. +33 1 48 06 21 84

A wine cave with traditional degustations and tidbits of cheese and charcuterie. This pretty shop and "snackeria" is totally devoted to smart and small wines, many with biodynamic preparations. It also welcomes fashionable events such as summer 2012's dinner with talk-of-the-town Japanese chef Maori Murota (see p. 23).

CHEZ BOGATO
7, rue Liancourt, 75014
Tel. +33 1 40 47 03 51
The most beautiful cakes you can dream of, with outstanding themes, such as the Sailor and Lula biscuit, decorated with a leopard bow; a mascarpone fairy-tale multitower castle; and chocolate fondants in the shape of fire trucks, dinosaurs, wolves, and stilettos. Plan B: LA PÂTISSERIE DES RÊVES (93, rue du Bac, 75007; Tel. +33 1 42 84 00 82), the "sweet spot" of Isabel Marant.

ÉPICERIE IZRAËL
30, rue François Miron, 75004
Tel. +33 1 42 72 66 23
A favorite of makeup artists like Tom Pêcheux, perfumers, and foodies, this deli carries the most exotic spices from all over the world in cute retro jars: leaves of lemon, pepper from Cameroon, or rare historic mixes; for instance, a hundred-and-twenty-year-old one from Marseilles called Epices de Rabelais.

HERBORISTERIE DU PALAIS ROYAL
11, rue des Petits-Champs, 75001
Tel. +33 1 42 97 54 68
Every time we pass behind the Palais Royal, we think of the late YSL muse Loulou de La Falaise, who used to mention this phytoscience apothecary in her interviews. Fashion people get their antifatigue Siberian ginseng here during the biannual fashion-collections migrations.

APÉRO

For those who might declare that there is nothing more antifashion
than a post-work glass of red wine, three words: Maison Martin
Margiela. Remember when they used to welcome you to their shows
in their laboratory uniforms with plastic cups of Cabernet?

LE FUMOIR
6, rue de l'Amiral-de-Coligny, 75001
Tel. +33 1 42 92 00 24

The bourgeois wine bar, lounge, and restaurant that fashion people
will patronize even if they are not totally convinced they should.
Too many finance-type patrons? Too "boutique" in style? Sometimes the wine, supposedly the big draw here, can be a letdown.
But it's central (by the Louvre), the martinis are served late, and the
food is always fresh and almost surprisingly delicious. A good spot
for brunch, too.

LE DERRIÈRE
69, rue des Gravilliers, 75003
Tel. +33 1 44 61 91 95

A family-apartment-style venue opened clandestinely like a
speakeasy in 2008, it is still highly popular with the Le Baron
crowd, especially since being celebrated in a *New York Times*
article. Shabby chic, with some decent salads and table tennis.
Find it behind an unmarked door in the courtyard between 404
and AndyWhaloo—the Moroccan restaurant and bar (with a
charming outdoor space) from the same owners.

CHEZ JEANNETTE

47, rue du Faubourg-Saint-Denis, 75010

Tel. +33 1 47 70 30 89

A stone's throw from Jean Paul Gaultier's HQ, this old-school, authentic-1950s café, complete with high ceilings and red-moleskin banquettes, has been transformed by its new young owners into the ultimate hipster hangout. A requisite stopover for a groovy "before," or an impeccable snack during the day. Plan B: Cross the street and hit the students' and assistants' fave dive bar, MAURI7 (46, rue du Faubourg Saint-Denis, 75010).

CAFÉ LOUIS-PHILIPPE

66, quai de l'Hôtel-de-Ville, 75004

Tel. +33 1 42 72 29 42

Difficult to find a more romantic setting, Amélie Poulain style, by the Seine, under an endearing *tonnelle*, with cool waiters and local patrons. Most appealing: the beautiful *petits vins*, like the dangerously gray category between rosé and white. For dinner with a similarly romantic vibe, walk a few steps to CHEZ JULIEN (1, rue du Pont Louis-Philippe, 75004; Tel. +33 1 42 78 31 64), the dreamland of Anthony Vaccarello and his boyfriend.

LA PERLA

26, rue François-Miron, 75004

Tel. +33 1 42 77 59 40

The infamous theater of John Galliano's dramatic brawl is still appealing to a typical Marais breed of stylish entrepreneurs, gay best friends, neighborhood art dealers, and fashion mongers. Same sophisticated nonchalance at these two terraces of the upper Marais village main street, Rue de Bretagne: CAFÉ CHARLOT (no. 38;

Tel. +33 1 44 54 03 30), a stronghold for brunches, and LE PROGRÈS (no. 1; Tel. +33 1 42 72 01 44). NB: The locals follow the sun—Le Progrès in the morning, Le Charlot in the evening.

OLD-FASHIONED PARIS NIGHT

To cheer you up after the temporary closing of the Hemingway Bar at the Ritz, if such is possible.

LE CAFÉ DE FLORE
172, boulevard Saint-Germain-des-Près, 75006
Tel. +33 1 45 48 55 26

A blurb from Karl Lagerfeld: "Without the Flore, Saint-Germain would not be (or won't be anymore) Saint-Germain. This is *the* ultimate café in the Left Bank. The reception and staff are unique. And I love their Nordic plate." The best hours to party with famous French writers, publishing big shots, TV producers, and cute girls in sexy minis and Chanel totes are between 11:00 PM and 2:00 AM. The business rendezvous start early in the morning.

MATHI'S BAR
3, rue de Ponthieu, 75008
Tel. +33 1 53 76 39 55

"Only for the elders," judges our thirty-something gorgeous night guide, Prada-approved DJ Mimi Xu. Well . . . it may not be fully attractive to foreign visitors and youngsters unfamiliar with the TV semicelebrities who patronize the restaurant and bar 24/7, but the auction-art-house curators and their collectors, both ironic and aroused by the decadent atmosphere, are still smitten. And yes, the red drapes and the sexy, glittery atmosphere can be appealing, even if you've never heard of Patrick Juvet.

HARRY'S NEW YORK BAR

5, rue Daunou, 75002
Tel. +33 1 42 61 71 14

Mimi Xu's verdict? "Tops. Not trendy, and that's what's trendy."
An early-twentieth-century American expat bar still haunted by the
memory of the Duke of Windsor, Hemingway, and Gershwin (who
apparently composed "American in Paris" at the piano downstairs).
Reputedly the birthplace of the Bloody Mary, Sidecar, and Blue
Lagoon. Major.

BAR LE FORUM

4, boulevard Malesherbes, 75008
Tel. +33 1 42 65 37 86

Another Paris insiders' secret, this wood-paneled cocktail bar has
been here since 1918, in the same family since 1931. With top-notch
mixologists, it also features two glorious vintage jukeboxes. For
businessmen accompanied by their rainy-day girlfriends—hence,
the discreet booths—and in-the-know fashion people.

ROSEBUD

11 bis, rue Delambre, 75014
Tel. +33 1 43 35 38 54

"Perfect for a margarita or a late dinner. Would it only be for the
waiters—in classy white tuxedos—it is a must-go!" says stylist
and lingerie designer Yasmine Eslami. Plus: the jazzy soundtrack.
Plan B: LE SELECT (99, boulevard du Montparnasse, 75014;
Tel. +33 1 45 48 38 24), with its famous cat, where sometimes the
400 Blows actor Jean-Pierre Léaud and real Jean-Jacques Schultz
characters are on hand.

NIGHTCAP IN PIGALLE

The former red-light district and Moulin Rouge area, annoyingly nicknamed SoPi (South Pigalle) is an anchor for the hipsters who have been gathering in its boisterous bars after dark since 2008. No fresh news, but still . . .

LE CARMEN
34, rue Duperré, 75009
Tel. +33 1 45 26 50 00

"Not to be confused with Chez Carmen (the 1990s drag queen hangout of rue Vivienne)," warns Guillaume Henry, the creative director of Carven. This cocktail bar scores equally high with LE SANS-SOUCI or LE MANSART in sheer numbers of cute boys and party girls. The décor is stunning: the former mansion of Georges Bizet, in all its nineteenth-century splendor, including a gilded birdcage, a candlelit grand piano, and columns and stucco galore. A fine place for trendy performances and DJ sets, with a popular book-swap club.

LE MANSART
1, rue Mansart, 75009

Having the same owners as LE FLORÉAL (see p. 27) means that fabulous David West's American-style cocktails are on hand here, too. Another bar boasting a Brooklyn-like ambiance, where table-football competitions, stellar cheeseburgers, and rotisserie chicken get along with absinthe, mojitos, bourbons, and Champagne.

LE SANS-SOUCI

65, rue Jean-Baptiste Pigalle, 75009
Tel. +33 1 53 16 17 04

Another genuine neighborhood bar upgraded to more sophisticated fare and beverages. Overcrowded to overflowing onto the sidewalk, with 3€ beers all over the place. Parties are improvised or organized with the occasional DJ or a rock-electro soundtrack until 2:00 AM. Reopens at 7:30 AM, when the bleak sun and street-cleaning trucks arrive.

CHEZ MOUNE

54, rue Jean-Baptiste Pigalle, 75009
Tel. +33 1 45 26 64 64

Opposite the SANS-SOUCI, this former small lesbian cabaret has become, since 2008 and the LE BARON team's arrival, (see p. 63)—the official den to dance, flirt, and finish the night in. Its vaguely neo-disco décor might be more a miss than a hit, the atmosphere insufferable or fun: it's entirely up to you.

AUX NOCTAMBULES

24, boulevard de Clichy, 75018
Tel. +33 1 46 06 16 38

Nothing trendy in this old-time café with its fragile, dingy charm and a famous concert back room. On its small stage, the singer Pierre Carré is a fascinating character, with his Elvis Presley coiffure and poppy-red suits, who has been busting his French and Corsican repertoire from the 1920s for a good forty years.

AFTER-DARK CLUBS AND HANGOUTS

Some seasons, Paris by night is exciting; sometimes it's just plain dull. It seems that all the 2012 nightclubs were on the downswing, and the public, left with nowhere to go, is eagerly expecting something—anything—new. Hold on. Should come with the next Fashion Week. In the meantime, here's a mix of seedy and classy current destinations.

LE 12 BIS
12 bis, rue de l'Étoile, 75017

Very elegant, very confidential, very fashionable, this nightclub was opened by stylist Victoria Sanchez. That's all we've been able to get so far, even from Mimi Xu, who won't clear up the mystery but declares her love for the place. Reservations by e-mail: 12bis@ruedeletoile.fr. Untested, but our rare insiders in the know are swooning.

LE MONTANA
26, rue Saint-Benoît, 75005
Tel. +33 1 44 39 71 00

Reopened in 2009 by LE BARON's (see below) André, *Purple Magazine*'s Olivier Zham, and Jean-Yves Le Fur (cofounder of *Numero* magazine), its mojo seems to have ebbed since its sparkling days in 2010–2011. The club's sexy moments and buzz are still monitored weekly on purplediary.com. Definitely the place if you want to celebrate Kate Moss's birthday (January 16), as she's considered a dear friend.

LE BARON
6, avenue Marceau, 75116
Tel. +33 1 47 20 04 01

In 2004 in a former hostess bar near the YSL house, André Saraiva and Lionel Bensemoun opened this avenue Marceau nightclub, and the rest is history. Its reputation has leaped over far frontiers, with pop-up or permanent locations everywhere from Tokyo to New York and Cannes. In Paris, the club is old news, but it still can be fun when a bunch of friends decide to take over for the night. Next step from Lionel and his new associates: the terrace of Les Docks– Cité de la Mode et du Design (34, quai d'Austerlitz, 75013), which promises to reenact Ramatuelle 1964 days and nights above the Seine.

LE CURIO PARLOR
16, rue des Bernardins, 75005
Tel. +33 1 44 07 12 47

"One of the best places for cocktails and whiskies in the Latin Quarter," says the accessory designer and flamboyant Paris character Yazbukey. Expect a taxidermy-and-other-curiosities atmosphere and a false speakeasy door easy to get past.

SILENCIO

142, rue Montmartre, 75002

Tel. +33 1 40 13 12 33

Well, of course you've heard of this one, the big hit since the September 2011 Fashion Week. Decorated by David Lynch, six-floors-deep underground, this private club was quickly celebrated by the *New York Times*, Hermès, and Gareth Pugh. Some consider it still hot; others judge it a bit vain with no killer host to jazz it up.

EXPERIMENTAL COCKTAIL CLUB

37, rue Saint-Sauveur, 75002

Tel. +33 1 45 08 88 89

Not to be confused with the kids' hangout, the Paris Social Club. The E.C.C. opened its first outpost on the Lower East Side in NYC in spring 2012 after the five-year career of this "speakeasy" in the Montorgueil area in Paris, plus three other locations (including LE CURIO PARLOR; p. 63). Their American-style cocktails have
been tested by the harshest critics of downtown Manhattan and deemed serviceable.

L'ÉCHELLE DE JACOB

10-12, rue Jacob, 75006

Tel. +33 1 46 34 00 29

A lush place for cocktails, not far from the popular *marché de Buci*. It used to be trendy, not much anymore, but locals and nearby hotel guests still like to hang out in the lounge, finding both glamour and typical *germanopratin* (in short: the posh literature culture of the Rive Gauche).

LE POMPON

39, rue des Petites-Écuries, 75010

Tel. +33 1 53 34 60 85

Still a good spot for a quick sip of hip in the rock 'n' roll part of the 10th district. Victoire de Castellane and Jean-Baptiste Mondino have mingled with young hotties in this former synagogue during a birthday party (sixty years for Jean Touitou, A.P.C.) or just for a last dance before a beauty-sleep call. Ambiance: "I ♥ the Black Keys" in the basement.

LA FÉLINE

6, rue Victor-Letalle, 75020

Tel. +33 1 40 33 08 66

Events: myspace.com/lafelinebar

Here you can watch Betty Page look-alikes with their Vespas parked in front till 2:00 AM. This rockabilly joint of Ménilmontant is set in a popular North district where students of the Studio Berçot (famous French fashion school) and fashion interns meet after indie rock concerts. One night, you might come across Gaïa Repossi; another night, it's Vava Dudu, the fierce multidisciplinary artist knighted by Lady Gaga.

SOIRÉES CLUB SANDWICH

Marc Zuffato and Emmanuel d'Orazio's nights remain your best bet for gay-pridey, old-housy, glow-stick-and-glitter, overdressed fun. Hit Facebook for current updates.

OOH LA LA

CRAZY HORSE

12, avenue George V, 75008

Tel. +33 1 47 23 32 32

The Paris *coquin*, on stage, always and forever. Camile Miceli,
then Louis Vuitton's style muse, chose to celebrate her thirtieth
birthday in this 1951 music hall. If you've seen Frederick Wiseman's
documentary about the 2008 makeover of the show, you know
already that the new one is choreographed by Philippe Decouflé,
artistic direction by Ali Madhavi, with skimpy, lovely costumes
by Fifi Chachnil.

LES CHANDELLES
1, rue Thérèse, 75001
Tel. +33 1 42 60 43 31

The institution for the swinger scene, it is oozing with decadence, chic naughtiness, or rude pornography, depending on your point of view. This club is another open secret in the City of Light's nightlife, like Madame Claude and Suzy Weiss (a legendary libertine). Just landed: a collection of LES CHANDELLES lingerie, described as classy, sexy, and selective. Only online.

FOREVER FASHION PALACES AND TRENDY HOTELS 2013–2014

Same caveats as with our restaurant list: There are plenty of other great options in Paris, but these are the fashion insiders' longtime *palazzi*, first-class hotels, and hangouts. Missing here is the very RITZ on Place Vendôme that Coco Chanel called home and Kate Moss her favorite private-party scene. It closed in summer 2012 for a twenty-seven-month, (rumored) $200-million makeover. (Reopening: Christmas 2014.) This has been followed by another dramatic "closed for facelift" at the CRILLON, place de la Concorde. Each will aim to reopen with an official "palace" distinction (the brand-new "exceptional luxe" category topping the 5-star ranking). In 2014, one of the hottest spots of the Paris Fashion Week should be the hotel of the CHEVAL BLANC in La Samaritaine, the former department store between La Seine and LVMH (the owner) head-quarters. Closed since 2005, it will reopen after three years of construction. Another forceful newcomer is the international PENINSULA (to open in 2013, 19, avenue Kleber, 75016).

Near Place Vendôme—Tuileries

LE MEURICE

228, rue de Rivoli, 75001

Tel. +33 1 44 58 10 10

Hands down the most international Parisian fashion palace. Its cinematic location near The Tuileries and Cour Carrée shows, its neo-rococo decoration by Philippe Stark & Daughter, its Valmont spa, the stylish *bar anglais*–like Bar 228, and the antipasti of the Dali restaurant are magnets for major designers like Viktor & Rolf, who name this landmark as their favorite venue in Paris. Meet the *Vogue* and *Harper's Bazaar* editrix from all over the world, as well as French and Hollywood movie honchos, plus one or two Russian billionaires.

PARK HYATT PARIS-VENDÔME

5, rue de la Paix, 75002

Tel. +33 1 58 71 12 34

Americans and Asians love this palace for its restaurant/lounge filled with natural light and its bright, modern decoration. The other perks are its convenient central location, its gorgeous spa (alas, guests only), and, above all, its incredible service: hands down the most friendly and efficient in town.

MANDARIN ORIENTAL

251, rue Saint-Honoré, 75001

Tel. +33 1 70 98 78 88

International luxe standards in a new five-star hotel designed by its owner, the famous Thailand group, with the help of French architect Jean-Michel Wilmotte. The décor is over the top, all marble and gold leaf, with the hostesses dressed like airline attendants. There are two restaurants for your consideration: the

fine-dining Sur Mesure and the Camelia (45 minutes/45€ menu).
A great place for a drink in the quiet garden, right after a splurge
at the nearby COLETTE and Balenciaga.

THE COSTES

239, rue Saint-Honoré, 75001
Tel. +33 1 42 44 50 00

Some 1995 nostalgics or the truly celebrity-driven choose to ignore
the dark setting and the questionable service and remain loyal to
this place where Yves Saint Laurent used to dine in the atrium twice
a week. Still the gem of the empire of the brothers Costes.

HÔTEL WESTMINSTER

13, rue de la Paix, 75002
Tel. +33 1 42 61 57 46

A hit hotel for American designers (Rodarte often greets its
European buyers here) as well as for the ultrachic fashion features
director of *Vogue* India ("Hi, Bandana!"), who loves its bourgeois
décor and central location. One of the draws is the famous club
sandwich, officially elected the best in town.

RENAISSANCE PARIS-VENDÔME

4, rue du Mont-Thabor, 75001
Tel. +33 1 40 20 72 17

This is a nest for editorial people from all over the world. A chain
hotel (Marriott) but with no corporate feel and a dreamy location.

Near the Louvre

LE LOUVRE

Place André Malraux, 75001

Tel. +33 1 44 58 38 38

A favorite of British journalists during Fashion Weeks (it is basically opposite the Carrousel du Louvre, where the official shows take place). You'll see the writers early in the morning, furiously typing their reviews, in front of the regal buffet at the brasserie. The cozy, dimly lit lobby is perfect for discreet advertising meetings.

HÔTEL THÉRÈSE

5-7, rue Thérèse, 75001

Tel. +33 1 42 96 10 01

Another British favorite in the rue Sainte-Anne sector, this comfortable boutique hotel is perfectly located, which makes up for the tiny rooms (recently modernized with good taste). Plan B: HÔTEL MONTPENSIER (12, rue de Richelieu, 75001; Tel. +33 1 42 96 28 50). Another prime location for a hotel that appeals mainly to New Yorkers or Milanese stylish buyers.

Near Concorde-Champs-Élysées

LE BRISTOL

112, rue du Faubourg-Saint-Honoré, 75008

Tel. +33 1 53 43 43 00

The grande-dame palace par excellence. A usual hangout for neighbors Fédération Française de la Couture and Condé Nast publications; therefore, a must for fashion power breakfasts and discreet afternoon business meetings. One Parisian tradition is to celebrate Easter with real bunnies in the garden, complete with a treasure

hunt and goodie bags. The hotel also organizes a monthly afternoon called "*thé à la mode*," a fashion show at the bar (Eli Saab, Stella McCartney, Ralph Lauren, George Rech, Azzaro . . .) with tea, canapés, and a special cake styled by the designer (55€, schedule and booking online).

SOFITEL LE FAUBOURG
15, rue Boissy d'Anglas, 75008
Tel. +33 1 44 94 14 14

A more discreet and less expensive option in the area of the Place de la Concorde. Fashion executives and designers with stores on Faubourg Saint-Honoré meet early at its restaurant.

HÔTEL SAN RÉGIS
12, rue Jean-Goujon, 75008
Tel. +33 1 44 95 16 16

Beyond the beaten path, this rococo *palazzo*, British-style, has been lauded as an ideal nest for an afternoon "*canaille*" tryst or a secret early-morning business meeting. Right behind avenue Montaigne and the famous couture houses, it's also an ideal location for a private lunch.

Near Trocadéro-Étoile

SHANGRI-LA
10, avenue d'Iéna, 75116
Tel. +33 1 53 67 19 98

This new, upscale, 81-room hotel with views of the Eiffel Tower, not far from the Trocadéro, is a spot-on example of world-class opulence. It attracts gourmets with its restaurant's surprising Asian-fusion cuisine, the glass-domed brasserie La Bauhinia, which can usually accommodate lunches without reservations. Stylish international visitors will love the Napoleon III grandeur of the building (formerly Roland Bonaparte's mansion, 1896), the secluded garden, and the Second Empire feeling of the private lounges.

HÔTEL RAPHAEL
17, avenue Kléber, 75016
Tel. +33 1 53 64 32 00

Head to the opulent Regency-style Salon Bleu or the Bar Anglais at this 1925 hotel for a real experience of good-old-time glam. Many golden-era Hollywood stars stayed and gave interviews here. Serge

Gainsbourg was a regular at the bar. The pseudo Fragonards and Titians still pepper the lobby corridor, and the place is now the favorite of Dita von Teese. During the summer the seventh-floor terrace, with its 360-degree view of Paris, is a must at teatime (Champagne and caviar).

Near the Marais

HÔTEL 3 ROOMS

5, rue de Moussy, 75004
Tel. +33 1 44 78 92 00

Probably the chicest address of the whole Paris Fashion Week. One- and two-bedroom 1,000-square-foot suites in the heart of the Marais, where Mr. Azzedine Alaïa moonlights as a hotelier. He welcomes guests and friends from *Vogue* Italy and the *Financial Times*, as well as his international family of supermodel-goddaughters (from Veronica Webb to Naomi). But the three apartments are also open to the public, starting at 450€. Furniture is by Marc Newson, Charlotte Perriand, or Arne Jacobsen, sheets are crisp linen, and house catering is heaven (only for friends, alas).

LE PAVILLON DE LA REINE

28, place des Vosges, 75003
Tel. +33 1 40 29 19 19

Queen Anne d'Autriche used to love this place as much as the cashmere designer Claudia Schiffer does now. Charming and extremely private, this hotel hides in a courtyard set in the Place des Vosges, the historic seventeenth-century square sponsored by King Henry IV (an über-romantic venue, even by Paris standards, with its authentic arcades and quaint candlelit restaurants). Technically, the lovely cobblestone patio is reserved for the hotel guests, but if you sweet-talk the waiter, you might be able to sit for a lovely gourmet tea—best warm *tarte tatin* ever—or Champagne al fresco.

HÔTEL DU PETIT MOULIN
29, rue de Poitou, 75003
Tel. +33 1 42 74 10 10

Opened in January 2005 in a former 1900 bakery set inside a seventeenth-century building, this four-star hotel is still a relevant address for many European visitors. Its kitschy-chic, quirky, jigsaw-and-wallpapered décor was by Christian Lacroix (who also went on to decorate Le Bellechasse on the Left Bank).

HÔTEL JULES ET JIM
11, rue des Gravilliers, 75003
Tel. +33 1 44 54 13 13

Maybe a bit too "boutique-ish" for some but highly recommended for its location in the Marais (near the fashion-insider-beloved restaurant LE DERRIÈRE; see p. 55), its late checkout times, its eighteenth-century fireplaces, and its program of artistic events.

Near Pigalle-Grands Boulevards

HÔTEL AMOUR

8, rue Navarin, 75009
Tel. +33 1 48 78 31 80

Although not the new kid on the block anymore, André's original hotel (a collaboration with the Costes chain) is still the place to stay for some hip stylists. They like the cafeteria downstairs, the patio, and the 20 rooms initially designed by friends of the house Marc Newson, Sophie Calle, M/M . . . Warning: Sometimes the greeting policy is akin to dealing with a *cravate rouge* (the famous security guards at the Paris fashion shows) without a proper invitation. But in both places, attitude is part of the game.

HÔTEL PARTICULIER MONTMARTRE

23, avenue Junot, 75018
Tel. +33 1 53 41 81 40

Not really convenient during a business trip, but this hotel-mansion, the brainchild of art lover Morgane Rousseau, is nestled in a secret passage high on the hill of Montmartre behind a black iron gate. Best part: the romantic garden perfect for an early-evening drink, the candlelit salon for later, and the artist-decorated rooms, which can all be booked privately for special events. Ask to have a look at the "Poèmes et Chapeaux" suite designed by the current director of Palais Galliéra and couture poet Olivier Saillard.

Rive Gauche

Near the Invalides

HÔTEL THOUMIEUX
79, rue Saint-Dominique, 75007
Tel. +33 1 47 05 49 75

The boutique hotel and gastronomic table of right now: fifteen rooms designed by India Madhavi with a great palette and fabrics, a staple for in-the-know foreign journalists (e.g., the smart writers of Style.com). Bonus: for a contemporary fine-dining experience, the two-star chef and owner Jean-François Piège's retro brasserie on the first floor, mixing French tradition and rock'n'roll beat around macaroni, lobster, foie gras, and truffles.

Near Saint-Germain-des-Près

L'HÔTEL
13, rue des Beaux-Arts, 75006
Tel. +33 1 44 41 99 00

This historical hotel (sometimes called "the French Chelsea") is praised for its "very Parisian and literary charm" by all the New York belles. Oscar Wilde's last home (in 1900, he died in room 16 of what was then the Hôtel d'Alsace). Enjoy the lovely swimming pool and hammam in the basement (Jacques Garcia's aesthetic), which you can rent for your own private use, when Johnny Depp isn't occupying it. Perfect also for a late-afternoon drink.

HÔTEL VERNEUIL
8, rue de Verneuil, 75007
Tel. +33 1 42 60 82 14

The main draws are not the nearby Musée d'Orsay or the Socialist Party's HQ, but Serge Gainsbourg's historic mansion across the street and Karl Lagerfeld's 7L bookstore, one block down (see p. 000). A quaint place to stay in Paris, luxurious and upbeat, with books galore to remind you that James Baldwin spent a winter there. Plan B: HÔTEL SAINT-VINCENT (5, rue du Pré-aux-Clercs, 75007; Tel. +33 1 42 61 01 51), a three-star spot favored by Australian *Vogue*.

LE MONTALEMBERT
3, rue Montalembert, 75007
Tel. +33 1 45 49 68 68

Another Rive Gauche staple for its publishers' discreet meetings (Gallimard's historic HQ is a few doors from it), its secluded decked terrace in the quiet street, and easy access to the shopping triangle of Saint-Germain-des-Près and Le Bon Marché Rive Gauche.

HÔTEL LA LOUISIANE
60, rue de Seine, 75006
Tel. +33 1 44 32 17 17

A more affordable hotel, preferred by educated stylists who appreciate this former favorite spot of Simone de Beauvoir, visiting jazz men, and 1980s Ford models (a then-unknown Christy Turlington and Stephanie Seymour spent a summer of castings here). It seems to be now a favorite hostelry for tastemakers like photographers David Armstrong and Jack Pierson. Warning: spartan! But artist friendly. Ask for the bigger rooms under the roof in a small apartment that could have been Juliette Greco's or Arletty's.

BEL AMI
7–11, rue Saint-Benoît, 75006
Tel. +33 1 42 61 53 53

Tiny, modest, comfortable, and friendly four-star boutique hotel in the heart of Saint-Germain-des-Près. Some will find it difficult to stay in such small rooms with their oversize Louis Vuitton bags. But those who travel light will appreciate the lingering old-Paris ethos. Plan B for fashion assistants or those on a budget: CRYSTAL HOTEL (24, rue Saint-Benoît, 75006; Tel. +33 1 45 48 85 14). Bigger rooms, plain, at under $200.

Parisian Tips

This is where the fashion insiders based in Paris would choose to stay if they were you.

HÔTEL DUC DE SAINT SIMON

14, rue de Saint-Simon, 75007
Tel. +33 1 44 39 20 20

An eighteenth-century mansion, nostalgic, discreet. Some suites with private terrace. Bonus: a friendly front desk, a lovely, leafy cobblestone courtyard with restaurant tables, rough-hewn stone walls, salons, and vintage paintings in the corridors.

HÔTEL DE L'ABBAYE

10, rue Cassette, 75006
Tel. +33 1 45 44 38 11

With a small courtyard and a pretty, secluded garden for summer, a lovely salon with a fireplace for winter, the eclectic bourgeois-chic decoration is nowhere more inviting than in the private lounges and duplex suite with private terrace. A gem.

HÔTEL RÉCAMIER
3, place Saint-Sulpice, 75006
Tel. +33 1 43 26 04 89

Far away from the fashion epicenter, this hotel *de charme* has recently been jazzed up with a sweet mix of neoclassic-fifties style by the owner of the THÉRÈSE (see p. 70) without falling into the gimmicks of a boutique hotel. Patio, free WiFi, late service, and view of the majestic piazza Saint-Sulpice.

Quirky and Cheap
HÔTEL CRAYON
25, rue du Bouloi, 75001
Tel. +33 1 42 36 54 19

A hit with fashion assistants, this very affordable and whimsically decorated hotel is ideally located: a five-minute walk from le Carrousel du Louvre, heart of the Paris Fashion Weeks. The concept is an "artist's studio" from the point of view of a hotel marketing company. Kudos for the free WiFi and AC and the friendly, really helpful staff.

MAMA SHELTER
109, rue de Bagnolet, 75020
Tel. +33 1 43 48 48 48

Another affordable address, a trek from Paris Center but über-hyped, opened under the advice of a French philosopher, with the decoration involvement of the two nineties French giants Philip Starck and Roland Castro. Fun minimalism (check the carpets), WiFi, and kitchen corner with microwave. Opposite is La Flèche d'Or, a beer-and-concert venue also dating from the nineties. A good address also for a remote and quiet Sunday brunch.

TAYLOR HÔTEL
6, rue Taylor, 75010
Tel. +33 1 42 40 11 01

A ten-minute walk from the Marais, in a narrow and quiet street, this hotel is a real bargain with its friendly rates of under $100 for a soundproof single room, its sensual, soft colors, neoclassic feeling, and complimentary WiFi.

BEAUTY
& HEALTH

HAIRSTYLISTS

The French are reputed for the quality of their hairdressing. So why did Parisian girls never really buy in to that three-blow-outs-a-week habit of yours, my dear American friends? In French, we call a blow-dry *brushing* (pronounced "br-ə-sheeng" . . . Don't ask). Single process is *couleur* ("koo-l-ʒːʳ"). Highlights is *balayage* ("ba-lei-a-ʒ"). Check out the landmarks below.

Cut

DAVID MALLETT
14, rue Notre-Dame-des-Victoires, 75002
Tel. +33 1 40 20 00 23

The most beautiful salon in Paris, in a seventeenth-century *hôtel particulier*. David Mallett, an Australian scissors whiz and the coolest boy in town, is always on hand, despite his prestigious editorial and ad work (Christy Turlington for Chanel, Liv Tyler for Givenchy, etc.) for his loyal customers, stylists, fashion writers, Eva Green, Natalie Portman, Charlotte Gainsbourg . . . If he's not, you can totally trust Barbara. A cut by either of them is the best souvenir to bring back home, with his magic Hair Serum DM027. Also book Laurence, a regular of fashion backstage, for a manicure.

JOHN NOLLET
Hôtel Park Hyatt Paris-Vendôme
5, rue de la Paix, 75002
Tel. +33 1 55 80 71 50

Set in Suite 101, decorated with the theme of travel (custom-made Louis Vuitton trunks . . .), the favorite hairstylist and dear friend of Chanel ambassador Vanessa Paradis is technically available 24/7.

In reality, at night you might be with one of his assistants, and appointments have to be arranged with Audrey: "Honestly, we've never had a request for a blow-dry at 3:00 AM." But it's "absolutely possible" to book an 11:00 PM hair-care appointment with night oil mask, followed by a 6:00 AM styling and blow-out. Schedule three weeks ahead for a cut or a session with Mr. Nollet himself.

STUDIO 34
34, rue du Mont-Thabor, 75001
Tel. +33 1 47 03 35 35

Delphine Courteille, the "fashion hairdresser," is famous in the Parisian beauty world for having been on Odile Gilbert's team, backstage during the Fashion Weeks, for many seasons. She has opened a new salon, already noted by *Allure* in its little-black-book pages and promoted by Sofia Coppola, in love with her dry cuts and her little white house hidden in a courtyard.

STUDIO MARISOL
33 ter, rue des Tournelles, 75003
Tel. +33 1 44 61 18 34

Marisol Suarez is a rising star in the Paris of beauty and fashion editors. This former artistic director of Toni&Guy, trained at the Jean-Marc Maniatis school, is a virtuoso of haute-couture wigs (for fashion-shoot sets) and dry cuts (for everyone). Modern, intuitive, with great standards, she is definitely worth a visit. For color, ask to see the whiz named Karima; for René Furterer hair care, ask for Shue.

ISABELLE LUZET

6, square de l'Opéra-Louis-Juvet, 75009
Tel. +33 1 40 07 00 96

Juliette Binoche, Emmanuelle Béart, and Laetitia Casta are some of those loyal to this gifted hairstylist, a pretty blonde herself, and her salon in the quaint area of Theater Edouard VII, behind the Opera. Ask her to tell you how the French crooner Serge Gainsbourg handpicked her in the salon Jacques Dessange, where she started her career, and opened the path for her into the film industry.

ATELIER DONATO AND DON CROSS

207, rue Saint-Honoré, 75001
Tel. +33 1 40 20 45 18

Cut, manicure, makeup, massage: one-stop global pampering is available in this cool, bi-level salon and spa. Ask for Donato himself, present every weekday here, including Monday, a rarity in Paris. Don't go with too-thin strands, though: He is famous for trimming very thick, dense hair, which will grow impeccably disciplined.

SALON MICHEL CATHOU-HERVÉ DUBOC

15, rue Boissy d'Anglas, 75008
Tel. +33 1 47 42 15 77

Not on the official list of fancy salons, but the French *Vogue* ad executives always stop there midafternoon for a quick fix. Ask for Sarah, the whiz colorist.

ATELIER SERGE D'ESTEL

78, rue de Vaugirard, 75006
Tel. +33 1 45 48 43 80

A nonfancy, friendly, and reliable place. Serge d'Estel has never felt the need to raise his ridiculously low rates, almost similar to salon chains (same décor also), despite the bespoke service. His cuts are precise, giving life back to even the dullest hair, empowering the features, and boosting the mood.

On Call

ERIC ROMAN

Tel. +33 6 27 30 37 79
E-mail: contact@ericroman.com

Fashion and beauty editors, as well as the 2012 *Vanity Fair* best-dressed Lea Seydoux, used to flock to his apartment salon by the Champs-Élysées. Eric Roman knows by heart the story of the Paris hair salons: "the sixties to the eighties, when Jacques Dessange was breaking the code of modern hairdressing, casting off rollers, working hair with fingers, drying like a beach effect, a trend continued by Jean-Marc Maniatis and Jean-Louis David (who came from the famous Carita sisters)." Eric Roman Emoi salon is now closed, but this maestro is available on call for a killer cut, as well as on Thursday and Friday at STUDIO MARISOL (see p. 85).

Color

CHRISTOPHE ROBIN

Hôtel Le Meurice, 228, rue de Rivoli, 75001
Tel. +33 1 40 20 02 83

Über-luxe and reserved for those ready to deal with major attitude. This celebrity and lifestyle "guru colorist and hairdresser" welcomes his high-end customers in Suite 128, first floor, an 860-square-foot "fashion spa for hair." Good enough for Catherine Deneuve, Isabelle Adjani, and Kristin Scott Thomas; good enough for you, right?

L'ATELIER BLANC

6, rue Mayran, 75009

Tel. +33 1 42 39 62 70

Frédéric Mennetrier has been in the fashion business for so long that he completely masters all the trends. He can launch them, and the major magazines and the fashion-show backstage will follow. This color-craft man loves to give advice in his glam black and white design salon. Sun-kissed blond or shiny brunet will equally catch light.

ROMAIN COLORS

37, rue Rousselet, 75007

Tel. +33 1 42 73 24 19

Finding John Masters Organics products in a salon can only be a good omen. This organic-premium colorist has been obsessed with natural and organic products since his herbologist grandfather initiated him during his childhood in Britain. He's always inventing new recipes from clay and olive oil to kick out the chemicals. His hair *mise en beauté* can last hours and seem pricey, but what a splurge.

COLORÉ PAR RODOLPHE

26-28, rue Danielle-Casanova, 75002

Tel. +33 1 42 61 46 59

A stone's throw from Place Vendôme and a *chouchou* of many actresses, whom you can see sneaking from his special back space. Obviously pricey, but priceless. Ask Rodolphe himself for a perfect color with his wonderful homemade products.

DES GARÇONS

217, rue Saint-Honoré, 75001

Tel. +33 1 42 97 57 91

A new gang of three hot stylists who came from Eric Roman Emoi and David Mallett. Their salon for boys and girls offers reasonably priced cuts, blow-outs, color, and highlights, with extensions upon request. They also boast buns (150€), as for a 1958 Diana Vreeland *Harper's Bazaar* photo shoot.

AVEDA-JOËL VILLARD
16, rue de Saint-Simon, 75007
Tel. +33 1 45 55 85 69

The Estée Lauder natural brand Aveda is highly respected in Paris. This salon, which is an official distributor, is a well-known and beloved address in the world of women's magazines: elegant and cozy, it is totally dedicated to the well-being of its customers. The hair care (by Monique) lasts ninety minutes, with a massage that will send you to heaven.

BLONDE BY FRANCK VIDOFF
12, rue du Pré-aux-Clercs, 75007
Tel. +33 1 42 22 66 33

A bikram yoga teacher, an artist, an aesthete, and a colorist maestro: All the blondes love larger-than-life Franck Vidoff and his tiny rogue salon on Rive Gauche. Recommended by his colleague Eric Roman, which means a lot.

DAVID LUCAS
En Aparté, 20, rue Danielle-Casanova, 75002
Tel. +33 1 47 03 92 04

His Haussmann apartment is by Place Vendôme. David Lucas spent ten years at the hair-care specialist René Furterer Institute. Obviously, he knows how to help distressed hair. Another go-to guy for highlights.

On Call

ALAIN SILVANI

Tel. +33 6 14 62 53 22

This colorist, often found on film and fashion sets, also visits regular private clients, having given Vanessa Bruno her rock-sexy blond. He comes recommended by brunet stylist and lingerie designer Yasmine Eslami.

Extensions

SALON DESSANGE INTERNATIONAL

39, avenue Franklin D. Roosevelt, 75008

Tel. +33 1 43 59 31 31

In a Zen atmosphere, this white salon is a reliable place for hair care (oils with massage and mask) and also extensions, a tricky genre that is perfectly mastered here.

Bangs and Buns

MAISON DE COIFFURE CHRISTOPHE-NICOLAS BIOT
52, rue Saint-André-des-Arts, 75006
Tel. +33 1 43 26 58 21

Famous for its *bar à chignon* (buns bar), a wonderful concept if you need your hair done in ten, twenty, or thirty minutes. You can choose from a sixties haute-couture look to a poetic, messy, "back-from-the-beach" bun for very reasonable fees. Courrèges-approved (the *maison* often partners with Christophe-Nicolas Biot, for pop-up bun bars on its premises, on the Right Bank).

SALON DIDACT HAIR
2, rue du Jour, 75001
Tel. +33 1 82 28 30 10

Another cool place, this impressive (three floors in a seventeenth-century building), totally green-conscious salon can give you real-looking bangs, in natural hair, dyed and hand sewn, in less time than it would take to cut real ones. Also a braids-and-buns bar.

Hair Care

LEONOR GREYL
15, rue Tronchet, 75008
Tel. +33 1 42 65 32 26

Her 1980 dry palm oil for hair is championed by everyone, especially Odile Gilbert, the queen of hairstylists in the fashion backstage. An oldie (say, forty-five years) but golden staple of Paris, specializing in color and hair revitalization with ninety-minute natural treatments based on plants (palm, magnolia, orchids . . .), customized masks and oils, at very reasonable prices (and with complimentary shoulder massage). Ask for Gilles if the great Leonor, and her precious advice, is not on hand.

RENÉ FURTERER
15, place de la Madeleine, 75008
Tel. +33 1 42 65 30 60
A two-hour scalp and hair-care treatment in a world-renowned salon/spa. During the first thirty minutes, they analyze your hair and scalp condition with a special machine, the Capilliscope. Then the spa treatment can start, with different, sophisticated massages after an application of nutritive essential oils or home serums, followed by a thirty-minute steam session and shampoo/styling.

Quick Blow-Dry

HYPEANDHAIRY
3, rue Taitbout, 75009
Tel. +33 9 51 84 28 08
A New York concept: 20 minutes for a blow-dry in a design salon with no appointments and at a pleasing budget rate below $15. Also available: low-cost snips, color, or extensions at membership fees by subscription. A girly girls' salon, which has recently added eyebrow tweezing, makeup, and blow-dry combined for under $45.

NÉO IMAGE COIFFURE ET ESTHÉTIQUE
28, rue de Maubeuge, 75009
Tel. +33 1 48 78 01 22
Another not-fancy salon, but Pauline is a blow-dry queen. She masters even the longest hair with her special Chinese brushes, and the results easily last three days, at the unprecedented rate of 30€, for long hair.

MAKEUP AND GROOMING

Not a service French girls are used to. The DIY makeup is the rule, even at preparty time. But these professionals are on hand for the high-maintenance visitors.

BELINDA KICANOVIC
At Don Cross
207, rue Saint-Honoré, 75001
Tel. +33 1 40 20 45 18 or +33 6 27 24 11 57
E-mail: belinda.k@free.fr

This lovely, former Stephane Marais team can take care of you in a quiet, relaxing room for a one-hour makeup session, day or evening, at reasonable prices (60€ or 80€). Familiar with the frenzy of fashion-show backstage, she can also perfectly work in tandem while you're getting your blow-out by DONATO's people. Easy to book (one or two days ahead should work), one of your best bets for a last-minute grooming.

On Call

CHRISTOPHE DANCHAUD
Contact: Serena Bonnefoy, serena@b-agency.com

The makeup artist of many stars and luxury brands, from Marion Cotillard for Dior Lady Black to Audrey Tautou for Chanel N°5 and Keira Knightley for Coco Mademoiselle. Available for private makeup sessions, but book him weeks ahead. You can also ask for one of his trusted assistants or another artist from this well-reputed agency.

MAJEURE PROD

12, rue Descombes, 75017

Tel. +33 1 46 22 70 11

E-mail: majeureprod@orange.fr

Raja Bouallou's agency is another go-to whenever a makeup event is scheduled in Paris and a contingent of experts is needed in an emergency, whether by the Ralph Lauren family or for a Crème de la Mer event.

CAROLE COLOMBANI

At l'Atelier (68)

Tel. +33 1 40 21 70 29

On very-special call. Alpha editors may want to book this five-star makeup artist, a favorite of Carine Roitfeld and Victoire de Castel-lane. If unavailable, the agency, well-versed in grooming-for-VIPs services, can send you other talents.

MEGUMI ITANO

E-mail: marc@calliste.eu

Tel. +33 1 40 26 76 77

Tom Pêcheux's former assistant can be all yours for a trendy grooming session proudly tested on supermodels.

In Stores

BOBBI BROWN STUDIOS

1 bis, rue des Francs-Bourgeois, 75004

Tel. +33 1 53 01 81 03

10, rue de Sèvres, 75007

Tel. +33 1 45 48 10 99

She celebrated twenty years in business in 2011 at the Paris American Embassy, at the same time that she was inaugurating her seventh location in Paris. A wonderful tip to get a professional makeup session is to take advantage of her "makeup lessons," available at her two studios or in department stores. Best bet is in the Marais, the cozy room upstairs where you can get a twenty-minute workshop on smoky eyes or rosy cheeks and lips (free) or full event makeup (100€).

BY TERRY

36, passage Véro-Dodat, 75001

Tel. +33 1 44 76 00 76

10, avenue Victor Hugo, 75016

Tel. +33 1 55 73 00 73

In stores, sophisticated makeup with these cult French products, from 11:00 AM to 7:00 PM. Pricey but spot-on. Two options: day makeup (80€) or special event (110€).

FACIALISTS

Two big names who have built in Paris what Kate Somerville has achieved in LA: complete supremacy in the red-carpet category. See below for a few other addresses no less interesting. To pamper you, snug and warm, far away from the frenzy of Fashion Week.

JOËLLE CIOCCO
8, place de la Madeleine, 75008
Tel. +33 1 42 60 58 80

This facial empress of Paris calls her job "epidermology." Fans like Monica Belluci call her an "artist cosmetologist." A former chemist, she believes only in customized skin-care routines and high maintenance. Her pet peeve? The lazy makeup remover ("three minutes minimum!"). Her massages are highly energetic, not for sissies. Her products are bliss in jars (not like her rates: Hollywoodian).

FRANÇOISE MORICE
58 bis, rue François Ier, 75008
Tel. +33 1 42 56 14 08

The other bold face (no pun intended) of the French facial aestheticians. Her method is called "kineplasty," a dry massage and noninvasive technique to "iron" out the face. She has started to train other aestheticians, who practice her method at more affordable rates (less than 100€ for 1½ hours), such as Claire Martichoux's team (three facialists per location) at LES PETITS SOINS (73, rue Legendre, 75017; Tel. +33 1 42 26 38 27; 66, rue de Vaugirard, 75006; Tel. +33 1 42 22 23 01; and 10, boulevard du Temple, 75011; Tel. +33 1 48 05 74 32). Also available: a low-priced, high-quality manicure.

JANE DE BUSSET
30, rue Pasquier, 75008
Tel. +33 1 42 60 23 53

Well, glamorous it is not. But this old-school institute is still the address beauty pros and socialites head to for an outstanding skin detox. A high-quality treatment nicely priced, a truly great secret of front-row insiders.

CHANTAL LEHMANN
175, boulevard Jean Jaurès, 92100
Tel. +33 6 79 34 95 74

Formerly responsible for creating the protocols for Sisley facials, used by beauticians all over the world, this gifted facialist is a specialist in strenuous face-muscle massages called "holifitness"—a mix of the many techniques she has learned all over the world: Thai, shiatsu, lomi lomi . . . ninety minutes of manipulation that can be uncomfortable but always efficient, especially if you get into the recommended once-a-month routine.

On Call

CHLOÉ VAGENHEIM
Tel. +33 6 84 07 11 65

First, it may feel as if nothing spectacular is happening, but then you get out, glowing and rested like after a week of vacation. Stunning lymphatic drainage of the face or the body that helps to detoxify and fight water retention. Count on sixty minutes for the de-puffing operation on the face, ninety minutes for the body.

INSTITUTES

The French version of spas, providing a typically Parisian ritual of regimens for body or face, usually in one-on-one, trusted, and long-lasting relationships.

AMBASSADE DE LA BEAUTÉ, BIOLOGIQUE RECHERCHE
32, avenue des Champs-Élysées, 75008
Tel. +33 1 42 25 02 92

Private and subdued atmosphere for first-class body massages and anti-aging facials, with legendary Biologique Recherche products (check the exfoliating lotion P50). Also available in this thirty-year-old institution are treatments rare in France, such as the electric massage with the Remodeling Face Machine, which uses three different currents. A nirvana of deep cleansings and facial massages favored by the likes of Sofia Coppola and makeup artist Tom Pêcheux, as well as by all the wise ladies from the front row.

INSTITUT ESTHEDERM
3, rue Palatine, 75006
Tel. +33 1 44 41 39 00

ESPACE BIEN-ÊTRE BY ESTHEDERM
At Hôtel Bel Ami
7-11, rue Saint-Benoît, 75006
Tel. +33 1 42 61 53 53

Another luxurious and professional venue where you can find high-tech and meticulous protocols for antidehydratation, anti-acne, anti-redness, etc. Therapists use E.V.E. peelings, serums, and cutting-edge sun-damage-repair protocols. Also, high-tech chroma-dermy with a Cellux device, to relieve skin aging or dullness.

MAISON DE BEAUTÉ CARITA

11, rue du Faubourg Saint-Honoré, 75008

Tel. +33 1 44 94 11 11

The September 2012 event was the arrival at this historic institute of its Cinétic Lift Expert, a machine, developed with a surgeon, combining ultrasound (for cellular-level massages), a vibration device (28,000 per second for optimum penetration of serums), three different LEDs, plus a spectacular pair of metallic gloves (woven with silver fiber) to conduct microcurrents. The Carita expertise is also available at the new SHANGRI-LA WELLNESS CENTER (10, avenue d'Iéna, 75116; Tel. +33 1 53 67 19 98, see p. 72).

INSTITUT LANCÔME

29, rue du Faubourg Saint-Honoré, 75008

Tel. +33 1 42 65 30 74

Follow American *Vogue* contributor and siren Plum Sykes. Indulge in a two-hour Absolue L'Extrait Facial with the very chic Karolina in a heated chair. This luxurious institute is set in the historic first store of the L'Oréal brand. Other draw: Thibaut is the star massage therapist for the past thirteen years. Caveat from the French *Vogue* beauty department: Ask him to ease up a bit on the meridians pressure if you are not a "no-pain, no-gain" kind of girl.

ESPACE ANTI-ÂGE FILORGA

20, rue de Lisbonne, 75008

Tel. +33 1 42 93 95 40

Specializing in the fabrication of fillers, mesotherapy, and anti-aging aesthetic-medicine products, this brand has opened an urban institute with cutting-edge and powerful (although not medical grade) regimens. The peelings (Glykopeel) are stunning, as well as the Cryolift and LEDs they are intended to be combined with. Also try the BB-Perfect, their new flash skin care, which promises a perfect glow in only a few minutes.

INSTITUT GUERLAIN
68, avenue des Champs-Élysées, 75008
Tel. +33 1 45 62 11 21

Revamped by the French star of decoration André Putman in white and gold, this luxurious institute offers classic but thorough skin care and body care, with hydrotherapy, massages, facials, and relaxation techniques. Also: The decadent weekend getaway of many Parisian girls is at the SPA GUERLAIN at Trianon Palace (1, boulevard de la Reine, 78000; Tel. +33 1 30 84 51 40). Wellness comes to you between laps in the gorgeous swimming pool and walks in the historic gardens of the nearby castle.

MENARD INSTITUTE PARIS
21, rue de la Paix, 75002
Tel. +33 1 42 65 58 08

Born in Japan in 1959, Menard is a poster-child brand for luxury and high-tech skin care, selling its stem-cell-targeting Authent cream at stratospheric prices. Its French institute (another one in Monaco) offers several luxurious formulas for face and body rejuvenation. Our insiders recommend Toshie and her magic shiatsu, deployed in forty-minute to two-hour sessions with bewitching names like Shirayuri, Kikyo, and Sakura.

INSTITUT DARPHIN
350, rue Saint-Honoré, 75001
Tel. +33 1 47 03 17 70

Classic treatments, famous for fifty years (like the "phyto-drainage"), and the wonderful fragrances of the essential oils that are the true core of the brand: These are the main draw for the actresses who love to push open the heavy door by the Place Vendôme and head to the back of the cobblestone courtyard, where the historic flagship institute and its five bright rooms are hidden. Ask for the signature deep-tissue massage.

APPARTEMENT 217

217, rue Saint-Honoré, 75001

Tel. +33 1 42 96 00 96

An organic, holistic, Feng Shui–inspired space in a beautiful Haussmann apartment, helmed by the wellness specialist Stéphane Jaulin and recommended by the likes of Guillaume Henry (Carven). The focus here is antistress, with energizing Ayurvedic massages and slimming sessions of thirty minutes/65€ in the Lyashi Dôme (a ceramic detoxifying box called the Japanese sauna).

NUXE SPA

34, rue Montorgueil, 75002

Tel. +33 1 42 36 65 65

The ancestor of face-and-body oil treatments, its Huile Prodigieuse Or is a cult product in France. Unpretentious ambiance under a beautiful vaulted ceiling in the quaint, cobblestone area of Montorgueil. Also reputed for its foot-beauty treatments. Optional tip from our friends: "Enjoy a glass of Sauvignon in one of the typical Paris cafés in the upper part of the street when you're done."

HOTEL SPAS

Recently, the palaces and five-star hotels have started to compete fiercely with new, outstanding, pampering spas. Bubbles of wellness decorated by high-end signatures, they are the most convenient places to ease long-distance-travel symptoms.

DIOR INSTITUT

At Plaza Athénée
25, avenue Montaigne, 75008
Tel. +33 1 53 67 65 35

An über-plush setting and incredibly stylish experience to energize and rejuvenate yourself with special house protocols, which can include: exfoliation with sapphire dust, 3-D stimulation of muscle fibers and energetic meridians, antistress wraps, and signature rituals with l'Or de Vie, active ingredients extracted from the vineyards of Château d'Yquem.

SPA MY BLEND CLARINS
At Royal Monceau
37, avenue Hoche, 75008
Tel. +33 1 42 99 88 00

Hammam, sauna, fitness studio, Pilates, and twenty-eight-meter-long turquoise swimming pool: This Parisian five-star hotel spa, airy and lush, has been given the Starck treatment to optimize the "wow" factor on 16,000 square feet. Mirrors, baroque chairs, and blinding white all over the place impress as much as do the customized My Blend skin-care protocols.

SIX SENSES
At the Westin Paris-Vendôme Hôtel
3, rue de Castiglione, 75001
Tel. +33 1 43 16 10 10

A Parisian outpost of the luxurious Thailand resort, its spectacular decoration features six arty white rooms and curved oak walls built in the basement. Green-conscious clients will appreciate the organic and holistic ethic and the Slow Life philosophy as much as do Daryl Hannah, Helena Christensen (allegedly loyal customers of the Thailand resort), and French *Vogue* stylists and editors, whose tip is to ask for Julie.

SPA VALMONT
At Hotel Le Meurice
228, rue de Rivoli, 75001
Tel. +33 1 44 58 10 77

Another Philippe Starck creation, managed by the Swiss-clinic brand Valmont. Think serious anti-aging, with a ninety-minute "lifting" process, to be followed by a massage with their signature rose/musk oils. Then, hop into the sculpted marble Jacuzzi.

SPA LE BRISTOL BY LA PRAIRIE

112, rue du Faubourg Saint-Honoré, 75008

Tel. +33 1 53 43 43 00

La Prairie, the luxurious Swiss cellular-skin-care process and products, has taken over this coveted spa. Flooded with natural light and a view onto an interior garden, even the premises have an antistress effect. The couples rooms are a hit, as well as the Banïya-inspired Russian wet sauna with Russie Blanche products (ask for the vodka scrub to whipcrack away your lingering jet lag). Bonus: By Terry reigns on the makeup menu.

SPA AFTER THE RAIN SWITZERLAND

At Hotel Saint James & Albany

202, rue de Rivoli, 75001

Tel. +33 1 44 58 43 77

Dramatic vaulted basement (from the seventeenth century), original regimens, Swiss-quality service . . . This spa has become a welcome stop, with its endless menu of body and facial care, its magically lighted swimming pool, and its hammam. Even the waxing treatment gives access to the peaceful amenities. The best? It's open to women, men, and children—totally kid friendly, with its chocolate wrap and strawberry-milk bath!

STYLISH MASSAGES

GREGOR SCHULTZE

15, rue Béranger, 75003

Tel. +33 6 80 93 59 06

Supermodels, LVMH staff, A-class actresses . . . Everybody loves this Zen osteopath, massage therapist, and Tai Chi zealot who merges anatomy, good karma, and 100 percent organic oils. Bonus: "He is so handsome and gifted that, between his hands, you can't help but feel aroused," comments a very chic Parisian.

MARTINE DE RICHEVILLE

At Institut Martine de Richeville

13, boulevard Malesherbes, 75008

20, avenue Bosquet, 75007

Tel. +33 1 44 94 09 38

At Spa Park Hyatt Paris Vendôme

5, rue de la Paix, 75002

Tel. +33 1 58 71 12 34

She is to massage what Joël Robuchon is to *haute gastronomie*: Ten golden fingers that come to you only if you get her cell number from Franca Sozzani, Juliette Binoche, or Carla Bruni—three reputedly loyal customers obsessed with her anti-cellulite, torture-like, tissue-pinching method. Curious? Test it in one of her institutes (also at the INSTITUT LANCÔME: see p. 99).

On Call

JULIEN MONTENOT
Tel. +33 6 50 02 68 62
Another *beau gosse* and your priority when the time comes for a treat. Overbooked, but if you plead a runway emergency, he should be there for you. Also a chiropractor.

JARING BLEIJS
21, boulevard de Strasbourg, 75010
Tel. +33 6 20 87 36 03
A very serious specialist of shiatsu, he is the favorite of Shalom Harlow, other models from the IMG agency, and many great chefs of Paris. On call or at his office.

NOUSHINE AMIRI
At Instituts Saara
5, rue de Medicis, 75006
10, rue Christine, 75006
Tel. +33 1 43 54 06 03
Other locations: institutsaara.fr
Five different locations in Paris (Saint-Germain, Victor Hugo . . .), but the owner, a generous and gifted therapist, is unique. Noushine Amiri excels at her Massage Harmonie China, rubbing you with two small pouches full of herbs for a supplement of targeted aromatherapy.

SANDRINE NICOLAS
At L'Art du massage
21, rue Ternaux, 75011
And on call: Tel. +33 6 73 19 98 17

A former makeup artist in the fashion world, she switched to her other passion, the massages of the world, using a mix of techniques from Swedish to shiatsu, Thai, and Ayurvedic, for a blissful, antistress effect. She can come to you anywhere, anytime on her scooter.

Worldwide Techniques

ASSA SPA
8, rue Christine, 75006
Tel. +33 1 46 34 59 08

A Japanese *salon de bien-être* that shows incredible respect for its guests, in keeping with its philosophy of *omotenashi* (*hospitalité à la japonaise*). It specializes in shiatsu, to prevent or cure any organic dysfunction. Restoring a fluid circulation of *chi* is the wellness principle here. With a warm welcome from the hostess, Mariko Hirakawa, and a killer massage from Jun.

CINQ MONDES
6, square de l'Opéra Louis Jouvet, 75009
Tel. +33 1 42 66 00 60

This luxurious spa boasts the broadest array of massages from around the world. The only downside is the frequent turnover of therapists, which makes it hard to come back to the same divine experience. But with specialties from Bali, Polynesia, and India, a chromotherapy hammam, and a Japanese bath, all with relaxing or energizing purposes, there's plenty to be experienced here. Come with an open mind.

THAI HOME SPA
68, rue de la Verrerie, 75004
Tel. +33 1 42 77 28 28

Pass the Buddhas at the entrance and ask for an expert reflexology massage without appointment. Be warned: It hurts. A lot. But it's a mandatory ritual for those who live on their five-inch heels. Also available here: twenty rooms in which to meet Thai therapists trained at Bangkok's famous Wat Pho temple.

HARNN AND THANN SPA
11, rue Molière, 75001
Tel. +33 1 40 15 02 20

In a nice courtyard behind the Palais Royal Garden, in a soothing, traditional, bamboo setting just behind HÔTEL THÉRÈSE (see p.

70), this is a great option for shrugging off your jet lag. Many options for impeccable Thai massages (Wat Pho, also), with wonderful home products (red-rice soaps, jasmine oils, house creams with kombucha tea and water-lily extracts). Express hammam: thirty minutes, 20€, for an anti-jet-lag express treatment.

On Call Only

DESBINA COLLINS
Tel. +33 6 14 96 15 39

Another five-star massage therapist, this Australian lady—a former fashion designer—is a master in Chinese acupressure, which she skillfully blends with Thai-Balinese techniques and deep-tissue massage, using special essential oils. The best hotels in Paris have her on speed dial for their star clients.

SUZANNE
Tel. +33 6 11 17 52 86

This sweetheart and gifted therapist was the star of the (temporarily closed) Ritz Health Club. A polymorphous talent, from *palper-rouler* (anticellulite) to Kiradjee (Aboriginal healing), from Ayurvedic to reflexology and Thai techniques, she masters them all and can adapt or combine them to suit your needs.

Endermology

KINESS
23, rue de Bièvre, 75005
Tel. +33 1 46 33 08 91

Think you could use a good anticellulite treatment before that
post–Fashion Week Harbour Island getaway? French girls swear by
the *endermologie*, a—yes, slightly painful—massage with a special
machine called Cellu M6. It can rid you of your bumps, at least for
a few weeks, with a bunch of thirty-five-minute sessions (65€) in this
humble, dead serious, but friendly institute. You can also deepen the
slimming results with precious help from a nutritionist, mind-body
coach, or sophrologist.

HAMMAMS

The ritual of the hammam involves scrubbing with black soap
(paste of olive pulp), then stepping into the steam room to soak,
moving from very to mildly hot pools (usually two or three at
different temperatures), ending in a cold plunge. No more than ninety
minutes, with or without *gommage* (exfoliation). Then chill out, get a
massage, and reward yourself for this self-love with a sweet mint tea.

HAMMAM PACHA
17, rue Mayet, 75006
Tel. +33 1 43 06 55 55

For women only and currently the unchallenged hammam of Paris.
This luxurious Left Bank outpost, open seven days a week, is 5,300
square feet of bliss, already in the database of many A-class French
actresses. Four-hand massages, *gommage*, lunch, beauty maximization,
or just mint tea in the relaxation room.

O'KARI

22, rue Dussoubs, 75002
Tel. +33 1 42 36 94 66

For women only, this über-luxe, authentic, Maghreb-style hammam/ spa is nestled in the vaulted basement of an eighteenth-century mansion in central Paris. You'll need two to three hours to enjoy the entire process, from steam room, exfoliation with black soap, and *gommage*, followed by cleaning with special Algerian olive-oil soaps, then a massage with essential oils that Karima Lasfar, the owner, fetches from the famous Mitidja distillery in Algiers.

BAINS DU MARAIS

31-33, rue des Blancs-Manteaux, 75004
Tel. +33 1 44 61 02 02

A stalwart of Paris since 1995, with hammam, sauna, relaxation zones, and also foot- and hair-care salon, with car service available. Still patronized by many stylists and fashion writers based in the Marais for its well-done *gommage*. Only caveat: Niceness is usually MIA, especially in the reception area.

LA SULTANE DE SABA

8 bis, rue Bachaumont, 75002
Tel. +33 1 40 41 90 95
78, rue Boissière, 75016
Tel. +33 1 45 00 00 40

Another gorgeous hammam and spa, mixing international traditions (from Bali, Malaysia, Syria, Tahiti, Japan), with great service in foot care and honey-based waxing. Wraps and massages use exotic ingredients such as shea butter, lulur lotus, and frangipani blossoms. After your hammam session, try the *modelage* with gold-colored powder made with musk and amber.

L'ÉCHAPPÉE

64, rue de la Folie-Méricourt, 75011

Tel. +33 1 58 30 12 50

A newcomer to town, in a swanky 8,600-square-foot wellness center set in a former industrial building of stone and steel. Boasts a Jacuzzi of swimming-pool size under glass ceiling, Pilates studio, massage, and mind-body regimens. The hammam includes two rooms, warm (100°F) and hot (118°F). Enjoy with or without *gommage*, massage, or wrap (moisturizing *rassoul*). Upstairs is a cozy brunch space where you may find Guillaume Henry.

MANICURES AND/OR PEDICURES

Each stylish Parisian needs her specialist in order to slide comfortably and beautifully into her narrowest open-toe Givenchy sandals. Since the professional organization of foot therapists forbids the promotion and practice of pedicures in spas, you get them in "para-medical" offices. Manicures used to be available only as a luxury service in the most stylish hair salons. Now they're everywhere, thanks to the new "nail bar" trend.

Right Bank

MANUCURIST

13, rue de la Chaussée d'Antin, 75009

Tel. +33 1 47 03 37 33

4, rue de Castellane, 75008

Tel. +33 1 42 65 19 30

Up to NYC standards, highly hygienic and tasteful, this lovely and reliable parlor has three addresses so far (including at PRINTEMPS,

64, boulevard Haussmann, 75009; Tel. +33 1 42 82 46 54). The Essie (L'Oréal) polishes are perfectly applied after customized hand care. Reservation mandatory.

VESNA NAIL BAR & BEAUTY
58, rue de Turenne, 75003
Tel. +33 1 42 78 12 58

Is this place a victim of its own success? The voice scoffed on the phone when we inquired if walk-ins were welcome ("This means you'll have to wait"). Nevertheless, it's one of the best mani/pedis of Paris, with a great choice of colors, including the 4-free (of dangerous chemicals) ones from trendy French brand Kure Bazaar. Open until 10:00 PM six days a week, clean and bright and ideally located in the upper Marais.

LES ANGES ONT LA PEAU DOUCE
254, rue du Faubourg Saint-Honoré, 75008
Tel. +33 1 47 64 48 24

This place has a nice way of greeting everyone, a cozy and clean setting, and a beautiful menu of "express beauty ceremonies" (thirty minutes each) for the face, hands, and feet (plus waxing). Impeccable mani/pedi (Kure Bazaar products an option).

NAIL FACTORY
147, rue de la Pompe, 75116
Tel. +33 1 56 26 01 08
6, rue Cardinet, 75017
Tel. +33 1 46 22 80 63
208, rue de Grenelle, 75007
Tel. +33 1 45 56 91 19

Trendy décor and highly qualified aestheticians imported for these

nail bars by the three Clarins heiresses. Also: gel or acrylic for nail bars by the three Clarins heiresses. Also: gel or acrylic for long time wear and pedicures in massaging chairs. The downside: Here, too, making an appointment with the haughty voice on the phone is mandatory. And the current locations are far away from Fashion Week spots.

Left Bank

SHU UEMURA

At Bon Marché Rive Gauche
24, rue de Sèvres, 75007
Tel. +33 1 42 22 33 49

The Bon Marché has become a serious anchor with its quickie nail bars, one by CULTURE OF COLOR (see p. 000) and a more recent one managed by the trendy Kure Bazaar. On the ground floor, though, this option is a rarefied and decadent experience, the opposite of the express mani. Come here for a real Japanese manicure that lasts an hour and takes place behind a screen in a regal red leather club chair.

PARIS/NEW YORK NAIL BAR

38, rue de Varennes, 75007
Tel. +33 1 42 84 02 39

Screams of pleasure came from the beauty bloggers upon the opening of this New York import in 2011. Finally, a bargain option for a decent nail polish change (5€) was available in Paris, alongside many other options, including Minx Nails art. Since then, the pedicure station in the basement has added an even cooler bonus to the place.

MISS CARLOTA

11, rue Princesse, 75006
Tel. +33 1 43 26 15 15

For those who fret that the old showbiz haunt (16, avenue Hoche, 75008; Tel. +33 1 42 89 42 89) may have faded after so many years, it has . . . and it hasn't! If you are not fond of the *beaux quartiers* institution, head to the Left Bank, to this new, cooler Saint-Germain-des-Prés institute, and meet a true pro, darling of the *Vogue* high heeled: Virginie. (Another new MISS CARLOTA: 4, place du Marché, Neuilly-sur-Seine; Tel. +33 1 46 24 08 08.)

Drop-In

CULTURE OF COLOR

1, rue Turbigo, 70001
Tel. +33 1 42 21 47 89
40, rue des Martyrs, 75009
Tel. +33 1 45 26 01 10
All twelve locations: cultureofcolor.fr

Another bunch of pleasant addresses for cheap and fast OPI nail bars, the California brand with 200 colors. Open late (until 8:00 and even 9:00 PM some nights). Appointments still recommended, but walk-ins possible. Also available: Spa Pedicure par OPI—CULTURE OF COLOR (196, rue de Grenelle, 75007; and 5, rue d'Ormesson, 75004). A decent foot-beauty experience in a comfortable massaging chair at a reasonable price (36–60€ with gel color).

SEPHORA NAIL BARS

70–72, avenue des Champs-Élysées, 75008
Tel. +33 1 53 93 22 50
22, place de la Madeleine, 75008
Tel. +33 1 53 30 84 90
75, rue de Rivoli, 75001
Tel. +33 1 40 13 16 50

The basic service of quick buffing and nail-polish painting by OPI and Sally Hansen is 10€, a complete manicure (buffing, cuticle care, cream) is 25€, with long-lasting (two weeks) gel at 35€.

On Call

MARCEA GOMES

Tel. +33 6 10 68 90 00

Difficult to get her on the phone, but if you succeed, it is worth it. Her foot-beauty routine is a must, tested on magazine stars like Emmanuelle Béart or Laetitia Casta. (Marc Jacobs is also reputedly a fan.)

SYLVIE OLLO

Tel. +33 6 23 56 84 41

The former owner of Capsules, a well-known manicure salon that is now closed. Specialist of resin for three weeks of fun, multicolored nails. Very affordable, friendly, and fun, with a strong taste for original colors: a tip from Yazbukey.

STÉPHANIE

Tel. +33 6 23 04 38 66

The queen of our foot-beauty section, she requires an appointment five to seven weeks ahead, as she is usually booked by all the high-end executives and fashion-magazine editors who fret about passing her cell number around too much.

EYEBROWS AND EYELASHES

Another rare service in Paris, where lash extensions are not popular and eyebrows are usually tweezed at home.

L'ATELIER DU SOURCIL

13, rue Notre-Dame-de-Nazareth, 75002
Tel. +33 1 44 61 51 51
12, rue de Littré, 75006
Tel. +33 1 42 22 10 12
80, rue Malesherbes, 75008
Tel. +33 1 42 56 06 06
Nine locations in Paris: atelierdusourcil.com

The only chain in Paris that addresses exclusively eyebrow beauty (no waxing, only tweezers), with semipermanent makeup and eyelash-extension options.

BOBBI BROWN STUDIOS

(See p. 95.)

Twenty minutes and only 25€ to explore the famous Bobbi Brown "*beauté des sourcils*" through a thorough lesson. Eyebrows are designed, tweezed, and brushed by the best studio specialists, who are also eager to show you how to do your own maintenance.

BROW BAR BENEFIT
At Sephora
75, rue de Rivoli, 75001
Tel. +33 1 40 13 16 50
70-72, Champs-Élysées, 75008
Tel. +33 1 53 93 22 50
21-23, boulevard Haussmann, 75009
Tel. +33 1 53 24 99 65
Other locations: sephora.fr

Warm waxing and/or tweezers for a perfect brow arching in eight minutes (express, 21€). With dying (three hues available), count fifteen minutes maximum (15€). Bonus: The operation takes place in an intimate space with perfect hygiene standards.

INSTITUT DE BEAUTÉ INDIENNE
Four locations, including
27-33, rue Philippe Girard, 75010
Tel. +33 1 46 07 44 67
67-69, passage Brady, 75010
Tel. +33 1 42 46 49 25

One of the very rare pros for threading. We haven't yet found a brave fashion Parisian who has tested these venues, but feel free to pioneer if you are familiar with the technique, a staple in London and a recent hit in NYC. Then reward yourself with a curry in one of the many restaurants around; if you choose the Haussmann passage Brady, it's not far from JPG's HQ and hipster hangout CHEZ JEANNETTE (see p. 57).

C MY CILS

50, avenue Victor Hugo, 75016

Tel. +33 6 11 88 30 63

A recommendation from the French *Vogue* beauty department, Elodie is a trusted specialist in Paris for eyelash extensions. Three options: natural, volume, or glamour. The procedure requires ninety minutes, but the immense perk is that she comes to you at home.

WAXING

Get back to the hammams—(see p. 110–112) for Maghreb-esque options, based on recipes with caramel, honey, and orange flowers. Below, a few other suggestions.

INSTITUT D'ARTOIS

38 bis, rue d'Artois, 75008

Tel. +33 1 53 76 22 20

No sign outside: This beauty parlor of a queen of beauty herself has no need to advertise, and that probably pleases its VIP patrons (bankable French actresses, etc). Best place in Paris, say some, for bikini waxing without pain (35€ and up).

SPA BEAUTY AMAZONIA

69, rue Condorcet, 75009

Tel. +33 1 48 78 26 35

This small beauty parlor is the best secret shared by the great Brazilian ladies of Paris. The warm welcome you receive echoes the quality of the care. Favorites include the famous Brazilian manicure (no water bowls but exfoliant gloves stuffed with keratin, allantoin, and other moisturizing extracts). The top-notch waxing is done by the expert Juliana, a doll with gifted hands and a big heart.

L'ARBRE À SENS

4, rue Montesquieu, 75001
Tel. +33 1 40 15 92 80

Test the traditional wax (honey, lemon, rose) at this new spa/hammam, which seems to have already seduced many stylish ladies in town with its discretion, cleanliness, and tasteful standards. Open on Sundays.

ANNICK GOUTAL

14, rue de Castiglione, 75001
Tel. +33 1 42 60 52 82
12, place Saint-Sulpice, 75006
Tel. +33 1 46 33 03 15

A famous embassy for rarefied perfumes, this institute offers skin-care protocols under a menu baptized "Boudoir," with anti-jet-lag massages and waxing options (including Brazilian bikini) in luxurious, old-fashioned décor. By appointment only.

E.P.M. CHRISTINE

26, place du Marché-Saint-Honoré, 75001
Tel. +33 1 42 61 60 00

Not a fancy place but a superefficient, quirky, mom-and-pop kind of salon, with old-fashioned foot-beauty service by Christine (trained at Dr. Françoise Dolto's school forty years ago!) and hair removal (with traditional wax) by her best friend since elementary school, the elegant Jacqueline.

FITNESS AND TRAINING

L'USINE-OPÉRA
8, rue de la Michodière, 75002
Tel. +33 1 42 66 30 30

L'USINE-BEAUBOURG
16-20, rue Quincampoix, 75004
Tel. +33 1 44 61 31 31

Marc Jacobs and all the sexy Parisians seem to have worked
out here at one point or another. Membership is required, but the
club may agree to enroll one-week visitors if properly asked.
A permanent card will give you access to the gorgeous vaulted
basement—almost dungeonlike—of the Beaubourg location. Here
you can channel Rick Owens in his new addiction: levitation yoga.

LE KLAY—SPORTS CLUB
4 bis, rue Saint-Sauveur, 75002
Tel. +33 1 40 26 00 00

This new designer gym has brought a hot vibe to the dull, old-school
training life in Paris. Five stories, 21,500 square feet, with hammam
and swimming pool and vaulted basement, in a vintage Eiffel-era
steel structure: The premises are gorgeous. A rare gym where Kinesis
by Technogym equipment and DVD players seem to get along.

PHISICS
16-18, rue Saint-Antoine, 75004
Tel. +33 1 42 78 97 27

Frédéric Vaché is a well-known fitness coach in the small world of
beauty editors in Paris, a veteran of the Power Plate and other waves
of high-tech training. Currently, his cutting-edge machine is Imoove.

With its "elispheric" movement (3-D), it corrects the posture by challenging your balance sense and optimally contracting your core and deep muscles, creating a sensation similar to surfing.

On Call

JEAN-MICHEL LAMARQUE

Tel. +33 6 33 51 86 86

E-mail: Lamarque, coachjm75@gmail.com

With his good energy and wide smile, Lamarque was enrolled by COLETTE (see p. 137) for a series of epic outdoor boot camps in Les Tuileries, summer 2012, but his urban training takes place all year long in the same public garden—a fun way to discover it. This exceptional trainer also works indoors and in swimming pools and advises about chrononutrition.

MARINE JACQUARD

1, rue Raynouard, 75116

Tel. +33 6 10 60 51 97

This dynamic and sensitive coach (also an actress, dancer, and five-year-trained reiki practitioner) teaches customized fitness in French, English, or Italian during private sessions in your home or at her gym twice a week, including breathing techniques and meditation. She is lauded by her clients (which include executives at Chloé, Chanel, and Bank of Rothschild).

YOGA

Not as huge a culture as it is in America, but Parisians are gradually building their stamina. A bunch of New York yogi expats recently settled in the City of Lights are guiding them.

YOGA CONCEPT
123, rue de Turenne, 75003
Tel. +33 1 42 77 74 67

A store with good karma: Yoga Concept carries the most upscale yoga brands imported from the US, handpicked for their high quality (organic cotton made in California or Canada . . .) or ordered as special editions from artisans in France, plus organic accessories, Indian jewelry, incense, argan oil . . . Pamela Levy is also your English-speaking go-to girl for anything yoga related in Paris.

RASA YOGA RIVE GAUCHE

21, rue Saint-Jacques, 75005

Tel. +33 1 43 54 14 59

Peaceful and inspiring, with its high glass ceiling, this center, bright and clear, has been voted one of the ten best in the world and offers every type of yoga class, some in English: anusara, Iyengar, kundalini, hatha flow, ashtanga, Mysore . . .

YOGA BIKRAM PARIS

13, rue Simon-Le-Franc, 75004

Tel. +33 1 42 47 18 52

17, rue Faubourg-Montmartre, 75009

Tel. +33 1 42 47 18 52

Perfect to fight the Paris winter, with the requisite 104°F and twenty-six traditional asanas, this school was founded by pioneer Marine in 2002 (ask for the ten-day discovery pass). Another bikram school by American Michelle has more recently settled on the Left Bank: BIKRAM YOGA RIVE GAUCHE (3, rue Campagne-Première, 75014; Tel. +33 1 42 79 93 51).

YOGA PLANETE

Contact: Anne Vandewalle +33 6 22 62 07 40

Class locations at: yogaplanete.com

Also at the American Church

65, quai d'Orsay, 2nd Fl., 75007

Every Saturday from 11:00 AM to 1:00 PM

guerillayogi.com

Tel. +33 1 40 62 05 00

E-mail: marc@guerillayogi.com

The New York fans of anusara yoga go to Elena Brower's studio. In Paris, they follow Anne Vandewalle. A favorite of supermodel

Veronica Webb, she has also been co-teaching at the Guerilla Yogi initiative—a wonderful, donation-based, two-hour community class in English, started by the LA expat Marc Holzman: For now, they operate once a week at the American Church. Check out the website or e-mail for updates.

ASHTANGA YOGA PARIS

40, avenue de la République, 75011
Tel. +33 1 45 80 19 96

Gerald received his first eight years of training directly from Sri K Patanjali at his Mysore ashram. With his wife, Linda, they offer very intimate classes, workshops, and lectures in English, in their studio with a view onto a lovely Zen Japanese garden (ashtangayogaparis.fr). Very serious and dedicated. Also: Ashtanga style at MYSORE YOGA PARIS (at Centre Shambala, 17, rue Eugene-Varlin, 75010; E-mail: kia@mysoreyogaparis.com). The practice is helmed by Kia Naddermeier, also a fashion photographer.

BIG APPLE YOGA

20, rue Dussoubs, 75002
Tel. +6 30 70 98 48

Another New Yorker who settled in Paris and decided to convert the city to the American culture of dynamic yoga, Janelle opened her bilingual studio in fall 2012. Anusara, ashtanga, vinyasa, Iyengar, jivamukti, pre- and post-yoga, plus many classes oriented toward babies, toddlers, and older kids.

THE YOGA FACTORY

21, rue des Filles-du-Calvaire, 75003
Tel. +33 1 83 94 29 08

For those who don't give a damn about the spiritual stuff, this new boutique studio focuses on the physical and mental benefits of its own hot yoga vinyasa flow classes (room at 89°F). Karine Vanot and Thibaut Tran Van Tuat, the two founders, want to appeal widely by fine-tuning the classes, from gentle and relaxing to more challenging and core building.

On Call

YOSHIKA OKABAYASHI
E-mail: yoshika.okabayashi@gmail.com
A reputed yoga instructor at Usine Opéra, who also teaches ashtanga to private clients.

PILATES

Again, not as popular as it is in New York, but this chic fitness has found its place among the rare physical activities Parisians can be addicted to.

STUDIO PILATES DE PARIS
39, rue du Temple, 75004
Tel. +33 1 42 72 91 74
The school is as close as possible to the teachings of the direct heiress of Joseph Pilates, Romana Kryzanowska. Philippe Taupin, the founder, has been teaching the technique since the late nineties and was the first importer of it to Paris. This studio in the Marais is still a magnet to a glamorous crowd of It girls and actresses, as well as the cool guys Taupin has converted to the technique, a rarity in France.

PILATES KEANA

11, rue du Chevalier-de-Saint-Georges, 75008
Tel. +33 1 40 15 01 40
E-mail: keana@orange.fr

Between Madeleine and Concorde, this bright, 1,500-square-foot studio is a chic place for Pilates in Paris. Some lissome French *Vogue* editors get their weekly training here.

STUDIO DANCE PILATES DE PARIS

18, passage de la Main-d'Or, 75018
Tel. +33 1 48 05 01 30

Another studio dedicated to·the memory and heritage of Joseph Hubertus Pilates, in its purest form, as passed directly to his student Romana Kryzanowska, who, with her own daughter, Sari Mejia Santo, has trained Mikael Pulcini, the owner of this Parisian Pilates hub.

COREBODY

76 bis, rue des Saints-Pères, 75007
Tel. +33 1 45 49 97 29

This studio boasts a dozen international teachers graduated from the Boulder Center of Pilates, Colorado, USA, and Romana in NYC, with physiotherapy or dance backgrounds. Fully equipped (Reformer, Cadillac, Wall Unit, Chair, Barrel . . .) and also offering regular three-hour workshops from the international guests.

On Call

NATALIE SHAW
Tel. +33 6 20 31 41 66
A Canadian graduated from Corebody in Paris, she gives private classes to fashion executives and politicians at their home or office. Both in French and English, with only mat and magic circles. Also: group classes at the ORA KINÉ SPA (60, rue Caumartin, 75009).

GYROTONIC

Done in a sitting position, a 3-D method of training your body with special equipment; a gentle but efficient way that will improve the whole posture.

GYROTONIC PARIS
5, rue de Charonne, 75011
Tel. +33 1 47 00 02 13
Juliu Horvath, the New York City Opera dancer and inventor of Gyrotonic, would have approved of this studio and the way it teaches his method, particularly focused on the vertebral column. A mix of yoga, dance, Tai Chi, and swimming, with a machine invented for dancers in recovery. Special stretching combined with core strength, executed on a spiraling pattern of movements.

ELEMENT PARIS
16, rue de la Grande Chaumière, 75006
Tel. +33 1 53 10 86 00
Pilates, yoga, and Gyrotonic in an elegant and friendly English-speaking studio (the manager used to live in LA). Also here: Gyrokinesis, standing exercises engaging the whole spine in a range of motions reminiscent of modern dance.

UMA

14, rue Choron, 75009

Tel. +33 1 44 53 61 13

This center specializes in massages (Ayurvedic, shiatsu, Thai), yoga, and Gyrotonic. It features four machines and offers special attention to pregnant women.

BALLET AND NEO-BALLET

Every well-educated French girl will take at least one ballet class before hitting her sixth birthday. Adults resume the practice, yearning to morph into one of the gracious swans of the Paris Opera.

FLOOR BARRE JACQUELINE FYNNEART

Studio Jazz, Centre Rick Odums, 54, rue de Clichy, 75009

Tel. +33 1 53 32 75 00

Feeling brave? Up for some classy French fitness? Follow the professional dancers here. You'll be doing some very tough stretching on the floor (soothed by a live piano). A sadistic and incredibly efficient method invented by the Russian Boris Kniaseff, taught in its purest tradition by Madame Jacqueline, a great lady of the twentieth-century ballet (15€). Back in NYC, you'll laugh at their Core Fusion stuff.

PARIS DANCE

Centre de danse du Marais, 41, rue du Temple, 75004

Program of classes: paris-danse.com

The French equivalent of New York Steps on Broadway (jazz, ballet, tap, belly dancing, tango. . .) in a historic seventeenth-century courtyard. Awesome. Stop at Café de la Gare in the cobbled courtyard for a green tea to reward yourself.

DAILEY STUDIO
71, avenue Victor Hugo, 75116
Tel. +33 1 40 67 98 57
A kind of ballerina boot camp, seventy-five minutes of barre exercises
and core focus, mixed with a touch of orthopedic exercises and a lot
of stretching. Imported from San Francisco by Kelly Dailey Vinoche,
the sister of the founder, it is all the rage in posh west Paris now.
Their baseline: "Get longer, leaner, stronger, and more fit."

WATER FITNESS

Parisians are fond of aquabiking and WaterBike. Aquabiking is
the French version of spinning, a collective class in a swimming
pool. WaterBike is the individual, upscale version to be practiced
in institutes. Sitting on a bike in water up to the waist, the effort
is amplified for the maximum effect on glutes and thighs.

LA MAISON POPINCOURT
4, cité Popincourt, 75011
16, rue de Verneuil, 75007
Tel. +33 1 43 38 96 84

Here, the aquabiking session (usually under ten people) has to be completed by an Iyashi Dôme session (the detoxifying Japanese sauna popular in Paris) and fresh veggie juice. Also, on the Left Bank: AQUA & BIKE (24, rue Monsieur-Le-Prince, 75006; Tel. +1 33 1 83 96 43 77), another private aquabiking center launched in 2010. Open six days a week.

ESTHÉTIQUE PARIS 5
43, rue Monge, 75005
Tel. +33 1 43 26 50 70

On the Left Bank, an old-time wellness institute, with WaterBike in individual cabins (with powerful hydromassage). A thirty-minute spinning session can be followed by a thirty-minute *endermologie* session for radical anticellulite action.

AQUAMOON
19, place Vendôme, 75001
Tel. +33 1 42 86 10 00

Another 6,450 square feet of Zen care, with luxurious décor and two marble basins. The focus here is on relaxing and slimming, courtesy of a staff of nutritionists, massage therapists, energy specialists, etc. But it is also another place to combine thirty- to forty-minute WaterBike training sessions and the detoxifying Iyashi Dôme.

PISCINE PONTOISE

19, rue de Pontoise, 75005
Tel. +33 1 55 42 77 88

Landmark of 1933, listed in the official *Monuments historiques* of Paris, this gorgeous, thirty-six-yard municipal swimming pool is a 4.50€ mandatory visit for anyone who can't miss one daily morning swim session. No fancy aquabiking here yet. You'll have to head to the other municipal PISCINE DES HALLES-SUZANNE BERLIOUX (10 place de la Rotonde; Tel. 08 99 96 33 88, local only). Less cinematic but a good array of water activities.

SHOPPING

We won't list the luxurious mono-brand boutiques—they're easy to look up online. Here a few spots for one-stop shopping if you'd rather take a quick look at the latest trends and follow the fashion-savvy of Paris.

DEPARTMENT STORES

The ultimate place to experience the European zeitgeist is LE BON MARCHÉ RIVE GAUCHE (24, rue de Sèvres, 75007; Tel. +33 1 44 39 80 00). The world-class department store celebrated its 160th anniversary in 2012 with its neighbor, Miss Catherine Deneuve. Always chic and witty, its selection is a must, from the lush *salons de mode* for womenswear, the two floors of menswear, to the third-floor bookstore under its gorgeous glass ceiling, with special kudos for the beguiling lingerie section. On the Right Bank, the most fashionable department store is the PRINTEMPS (64, boulevard Haussmann, 75009; Tel. +33 1 42 82 50 00), with star buyer Maria Luisa's designer shop within a shop (MARIA LUISA PRINTEMPS, 2nd Fl.; Tel. + 33 1 42 82 41 07). Nearby, its historic "frenemy," LES GALERIES LAFAYETTE (40, boulevard Haussmann, 75009; Tel. +33 1 42 82 34 56), is more driven by youth and street fashion, as well as its special devotion to contemporary art (visit the Galerie des Galeries). Farther on, in the secluded and conservative 16th arrondissement, is FRANK ET FILS (80, rue de Passy, 75016; Tel. +33 1 44 14 38 00), which is slowly dusting off years of blindness to cool trends. Last: the absolute favorite for beauty, lingerie, and cheap clothing basics, religiously visited by worldwide fans, is MONOPRIX (50, rue de Rennes, 75006; Tel. +33 1 45 48 18 08. All locations on monoprix.fr).

FASHION MULTILABEL STORES

COLETTE

213, rue Saint-Honoré, 75001

Tel. +33 1 55 35 33 90

For sixteen years at the top of the world's trendy-stores list, this must-be-visited emporium is a Paris landmark: a tourist magnet, cultural center, and fashion sanctuary, ever changing and gimmicky at the same time. International street culture and in-demand jewelry sit on the first floor; the luxe designers for boys and girls are upstairs, with the wittiest items of the season from Givenchy, Gareth Pugh, Marc Jacobs, Jil Sander, Valentino, Jeremy Scott, Comme des Garçons, or Junya Watanabe (CDG is the personal signature look of buzzing Sarah, owner Colette's daughter and soul of the temple). The Beauty Box, with its exclusive international brands, is on the second floor. Art exhibitions take place in the gallery on the mezzanine. In the basement, the Water Bar and its menu for weight-conscious gourmets is still the favorite canteen of the chic rue Saint-Honoré shoppers (see p. 14).

L'ÉCLAIREUR

40, rue de Sevigné, 75003

Tel. +33 1 48 87 10 22

10, rue Hérold, 75001

Tel. +33 1 40 41 09 89

10, rue Boissy d'Anglas, 75008

Tel. +33 1 53 43 03 70

LE ROYAL ÉCLAIREUR

Concept store at Royal Monceau-Raffles

39–41, avenue Hoche, 75008

Tel. +33 1 53 43 03 70

Armand Hadida, founder of L'ÉCLAIREUR, is another major actor in the Paris shopping scene, an early ambassador of the conceptual Anvers and Tokyo designers of the 1980s. From Martin Margiela to Ann Demeulemeester, his tastes have remained constant while his empire was expanding from the Marais to the Place de la Concorde. Each store has its own ambiance, usually intense: a hidden cavern for cutting-edge designers on rue Hérold, Piero Fornasetti's dedicated fantasy at the restaurant on rue Boissy d'Anglas, the gem kingdom of rue de Sévigné. The exceptional quality of the sales clerks, knowledgeable and darn serious, is a major attraction. Check out also 12, rue Malher, 75004, for menswear, jewelry, and fragrances.

MONTAIGNE MARKET
57, avenue Montaigne, 75008
Tel. +33 1 42 56 58 58

A minimal décor graces Liliane Jossua's swaggering, multibrand boutique in the Triangle d'Or (the traditional area of luxurious fashion houses between the Champs-Élysées, avenue Montaine, and avenue Georges V, virtually set on fire for Fashion's Night Out, September 6, and the Vendanges Montaigne, a biennial Champagne block party). At this store—allegedly the favorite shopping stop of Paris Hilton—institutional luxe brands are peppered with emerging and racy designers. T-shirts, jeans, and gowns are treated like equals, as in the celebrities' closets, which inspire the culture of the boutique and its website (with posts such as "Dress Like Katie Holmes"). A great source of accessories (shoes and jewelry) and many exclusives.

MERCI
111, boulevard Beaumarchais, 75003
Tel. +33 1 42 77 00 33

A 16,000-square-foot, multifloor store in a historic mansion with a charity goal (a percentage of its profits goes to an organization helping children). This bazaar, founded by the well-known Marie France and the late Bernard Cohen, has a neo-industrial loft décor and mixes decoration objects, young designers' jewelry, tchotchkes, home accessories, easygoing fashion, and vintage furniture. "I rarely shop in Paris," comments Isabel Marant, "but I'm always happy to come here. I love the space, the idea that you can buy in one place some clothes, flowers, or vintage plates. The charity aspect is very important to me, too." With a tea salon for scrumptious small bites catered all day long. Check the kids' concept emporium from the same family: BONTON (5, boulevard des Filles-du-Calvaire, 75003; Tel. +33 1 42 72 34 69).

L'ESPIONNE
2, place de La Porte-Maillot, 75017
Tel. +33 1 40 68 23 32
A bit off the beaten path but a good spot for easy-wearing and international luxe designers, handpicked with great taste for thirty years by Claudine Barnabé, the founder. Besides the politically correct (Balenciaga, Céline, Alexander Wang, Proenza Schouler . . .), she pays attention to the blossoming names (the new hit kid from NYC, Prabal Gurung, sold his first collections here, as Peter Pilotto, from the London runways, does currently). Lately, L'ESPIONNE underwent a revamping of its now 2,500-square-foot space in the basement of the 1970s Palais des Congrès.

SPREE
16, rue Lavieuville, 75018
Tel. +33 1 42 23 41 40
Twelve years of hard work by Roberta Oprandi (stylist) and Bruno Hadjadj (artist) have put this creative spot on the map of those who

like to get off the beaten path: local artists, actresses, musicians, freethinkers. Trendy fashion (Acne, Isabel Marant, Tsumori Chisato) sits next to vintage high-end designers from the 1950s to the 1980s, contemporary art exhibitions, and hit accessories (Marc by Marc Jacobs, Comme des Garçons).

FRENCHTROTTERS

128, rue Vieille-du-Temple, 75004
Tel. +33 1 44 61 00 14

Check out the new 2,150-square-foot flagship location of this dynamic and stylish multilabel store of the upper Marais, which opened its first spot seven years ago (still there: 30, rue de Charonne, 75011; Tel. +33 1 48 00 84 35). From their travels all over the world, Carole and Clarent Dehlouz put together a savvy mix of menswear, womenswear, housewares, accessories, well-crafted objects, and a stylish selection of brands they like to collaborate with, like Alden and Veja. Their collections are dedicated to the whole family (also a kids' store, 28, rue de Charonne, 75011; Tel. +33 1 43 57 04 09).

SHINE

15, rue de Poitou, 75003
Tel. +33 1 48 05 80 10

Vinci D'Elia, the very opinionated owner and trailblazer of the upper Marais, has been selecting designer collections since 1991 for her store, a former nineteenth-century chemist shop. Brands like Carven, Diane von Furstenberg, and Acne sit side by side with Alexander Wang, Marc by Marc Jacobs, Helmut Lang, and Mulberry bags or Opening Ceremony shoes. She also produces her own collection of separates, Shine, to mix and match.

RA

14, rue de la Corderie, 75003
Tel. +33 1 42 74 04 07

An outpost of the Anvers store, opened three years ago by two former students of the famous fashion school. Their Paris boudoir mixes vintage pieces by YSL, Paco Rabanne, Laura Ashley, or Mugler, the podium-confirmed hot boys like Gareth Pugh, and many other whimsical collections by Bernhard Willhelm, Jeremy Scott, Kokon to Zai, Juun.J, as well as handmade creative costume jewelry. Regular events and concerts are announced on their Facebook page.

PIGALLE BOUTIQUE

7, rue Henry-Monnier, 75017
Tel. +33 1 48 78 59 74

PLG BY PIGALLE

At Les Docks–Cité de la Mode et du Design
34, quai d'Austerlitz, 75013

A very well-curated albeit tiny store opened by a member of an artistic collective, Stéphane Ashpool, in 2008. Within its concrete walls: edgy Japanese and streetwear brands but also high-end designers like Rick Owens (get one of those long gray tees in a men's size), Felipe Oliveira Baptista, and its own brand, Pigalle.

AB 33

33, rue Charlot, 75003
Tel. +33 1 42 71 02 82

A small, ten-year-old, neighborhood multilabel shop by Agathe Buchotte. Feminine and perky with its love of gleeful prints (not a Paris thing) to be mixed up with casual wear or jeans. Lately, the racks held the likes of Tsumori Chisato, Notify, Philip Lim 3.1, and Forte Forte. Also lingerie and creative jewelry.

APC SURPLUS

20, rue André-del-Sarte, 75018

Tel. +33 1 42 62 10 88

A pilgrimage to Montmartre is on the to-do list of the fashion smart. Here you'll find stock from last season of famous brand Jean Touitou at almost half price. Splurge, then head across the street to the CHÉRI BIBI (15, rue André-del-Sarte, 75018; Tel. +33 1 42 54 88 96), another *bobo brocante*-like restaurant with a typical cool crowd of neighbors.

SHOES AND ACCESSORIES

Department stores (see p. 136) are still the most popular places to get shoes and bags in Paris. But lately, the multibrand stores have put themselves on the map.

LOBATO

6, rue Malher, 75004

Tel. +33 1 48 87 68 14

A gem for accessory addicts. Miguel Lobato selects only the best bags and shoes from the trendiest brands. Depending on the season: Pierre Hardy, Balenciaga, Martin Margiela, Michel Vivien, Lanvin, Chloé. Check his website for the current collections displayed in his beautifully installed boudoir of the Marais.

BIONDINI

26 and 78, avenue des Champs-Élysées, 75008

Tel. +33 1 45 62 27 40

A legendary glam-luxe fetishists' paradise, this store has specialized since the '80s in very, very high heels, caked with glitter—or not:

Alexander McQueen, Chloé, Lanvin, Fendi, Valentino, Alaïa, Versace . . . Stop by the two Champs-Élysées stores or the Biondini shops in the GALERIES LAFAYETTE (see p. 136) or LE BON MARCHÉ (see p. 136) and you'll get that secret, sexy, Parisian DNA code you were looking for in a flash.

58M.

58, rue Montmartre, 75002
Tel. +33 1 40 26 61 01

Here "style" rhymes with "comfort." A mix of not-to-be-missed fashion hits, such as Marc by Marc Jacobs or Repetto, and more exotic or emerging brands to be discovered if you're a no-nonsense walker, like the stylish flats of Michel Vivien, K Jacques, Church. Pick up one of those smart pouches from Comme des Garçons, a turquoise python-skin shoulder bag from Philippe Roucou, or a unique piece in salvaged leather by arty Pierre Rioufol.

KABUKI

13, rue de Turbigo, 75002
Tel. +33 1 42 36 44 34

Marc by Marc Jacobs, Surface to Air, Repetto, Opening Ceremony, Acne, See by Chloé . . . The multilabel store by designer Barbara Bui in the rue Etienne-Marcel area is still a good source for the season's footwear of choice. Check also the accessories to high-end womenswear brands across the street (from Proenza Schouler to Costume National) at the a women's store (25, rue Étienne-Marcel, 75001; Tel. +33 1 42 33 55 65).

IRIS

28, rue de Grenelle, 75007
Tel. +33 1 42 22 89 81

Since 2000, this producer of high-end shoes for fashion labels has been helping on the retail side with its own stores, opened in Paris, Milan, London, Moscow, and New York. Fashion cognoscenti still head to rue de Grenelle to find the new collections of Jil Sander, Chloé, Marc Jacobs, Michael Kors, and the too rare Veronique Branquinho.

HOD

104, rue Vieille-du-Temple, 75003
Tel. +33 9 53 15 83 34

Here you'll find the best and most up-to-date of the international creative jewelry crowd, all gathered in a Marais, boudoir-like accessories boutique. Valérie Hajage (formerly of Céline) mixes Indian scarves, trendy bags, stackable golden rings, and other treasures from the cool kids, including Pamela Love and Eddie Borgo, as well as Delfina Delettrez, and twenty others.

EXCLUSIVE AND VINTAGE JEWELRY

American fashion girls have been trading their best addresses with their Parisian correspondents for years. In exchange, we've asked our French friends to list the obvious and the secret in Paris, plus a few newcomers.

LYDIA COURTEILLE

231, rue Saint-Honoré, 75001
Tel. +33 1 42 61 11 71

"She has the genius of the jewel. I love her taste 100 percent," advises Karl Lagerfeld. Her client list (check it out online) is as impressive as her own limited editions, imaginary gardens of rare gems and baroque visions. Lydia Courteille's bestiary is wild, inspired by her trips to the Amazon and beyond. Also an antique jewelry dealer, she stocks some great vintage (Pomodoro, Boivin).

DARY'S

362, rue Saint-Honoré, 75001
Tel. +33 1 42 60 95 23

A store run by three generations of gemologist women since 1932, carrying beautiful vintage jewelry from the eighteenth century to contemporary. Crammed on the shelves and in the drawers are outstanding items of Victorian and gilded-era splendor, as well as lots of secondhand jewels. A must-stop on any New York It girl's list, including the Olsen sisters.

GALERIE NAÏLA DE MONBRISON

6, rue de Bourgogne, 75007

Tel. +33 1 47 05 11 15

This gallery comes highly praised by jeweler and girl-about-town Aurélie Bidermann. In her tiny space, Naïla de Monbrison offers her vision of jewelry at the crossroads with the art world, far, far away from your dull diamond ring. She follows her roster of creators like an art dealer. During her four annual exhibitions, she blends contemporary jewelry and exceptional ethnic traditions, with a preference for the boldest and most bewitching pieces, such as those by Violaine Febvret. On your way, stop at AURÉLIE BIDERMANN's own boutique (55 bis, rue des Saints-Pères, 75006; Tel. +33 1 45 48 43 14), a paragon of contemporary casual chic.

WHITE BIRD

38, rue du Mont Thabor, 75001

Tel. +33 1 58 62 25 86

A blond, quiet, modern space near Frédéric Malle's perfume boutique, perfect for showcasing jewelers from Europe, America, and all over the world, with prices starting at 150€ and reaching into the thousands. You'll be invited to drink tea, sit on a sofa, chat, and try things on. You can also just stop by to admire the exclusives, like the creations, all diamonds and 22-karat gold, from Hollywood darling Cathy Waterman.

IBU GALLERY
1, rue de Valois, 75011
Tel. +33 1 42 60 06 41

Under the arcades of the Palais Royal gardens, this is the brainchild of Irena Borzena Ustjanowski, a designer, artist, and architect who set up this sanctuary for jeweler-artists before passing away in 2002. Her love for exceptional, handcrafted pieces is still vivid in the current selection, presented among bronze sculptures, ranging from Ted Muehling to Athéna Poilâne (IBU's daughter) and Jean Grisoni. "Skin," IBU used to say, "is far more precious than diamonds."

LOUVRE DES ANTIQUAIRES
2, place du Palais Royal, 75001
Tel. +33 1 42 97 27 27
Browse online: louvre-antiquaires.com

You'll find great secondhand, cast-off family jewelry with perfect pedigrees here. Start at BRUNO PÉPIN (27, allée Boulle; Tel. +33 1 42 60 20 97), which recently exhibited stunning rings by Boucheron, Van Cleef and Arpels, and diamond necklaces by Fred. Or at BGC-BERNARD GRASSIN-CHAMPERNAUD (16, allée Boulle; Tel. +33 1 42 61 35 10) with its recent windows featuring Hermès and Chopard items. Or check out the cute diamond solitaires at VALÉRIE DANENBERG (3, allée Boulle; Tel. +33 1 42 60 19 59).

CASOAR
15, rue Boissy d'Anglas, 75008
Tel. +33 1 47 42 69 51

Everything looks vintage, but everything is brand new. Costume jewelry, with rings à la Buccelatti, earrings, necklaces, and "vanities," are sold in very limited editions. A notable address for thirty years, recommended by Sylvie Yeu, edgy *grande dame de Paris*.

PERFUMES

The world of perfumers is rich and welldocumented in France. You may want to visit some of them in their own stores, like the famous EDITIONS DE PARFUMS FRÉDÉRIC MALLE, the star initiator of the niche-fragrances revival, who "publishes" the best perfumers under his label (3 addresses in Paris, including 21, rue du Mont-Thabor, 75001; Tel. +33 1 42 22 16 89 and 37, rue de Grenelle, 75007; Tel. +33 1 42 22 76 40). Also: MAISON FRANCIS KURKDJIAN, 5, rue d'Alger, 75001, Tel. +33 1 42 60 07 07; LES SALONS DU PALAIS-ROYAL SHISEIDO-SERGE LUTENS, 25, rue de Valois, 75001, Tel. +33 1 49 27 09 09; LUBIN (since 1798!), 21, rue des Canettes, 75006; Tel. +33 1 43 29 52 42. Below, a few new concept stores.

JOVOY
4, rue de Castiglione, 75011
Tel. +33 1 40 20 06 19

Near Place Vendôme, opened by François Hénin, this embassy represents sixty-something niche brands, in a beautiful and pure décor of wood, steel, leather, and glass cases. From Rancé (Napoléon's perfumer) and fragrance masters old enough to have bewitched Marie Antoinette, to Heeley, Poiray, Jacques Fath,

Piguet, Frapin, and Grossmith. Come here to be properly initiated into the *haute parfumerie* concept.

NOSE
20, rue Bachaumont, 75002
Tel. +33 1 40 26 46 03

A clan of well-known professionals opened this 1,880-square-foot perfumery in 2012. The concept: A "scientific" diagnosis, based on your previous choices, helps you figure out what your perfume of the day should be, from among fifty brands available. These vary from the most famous (Diptyque, Acqua di Parma, Penhaligon's . . .) to the very niche.

SENS UNIQUE PARFUMS
13, rue du Roi de Sicile, 75003
Tel. +33 1 71 50 30 09

Thirty brands are displayed in this niche perfumery that sells the best rare fragrances, like the ones by Laboratorio Olfattivo, Maison Francis Kurkdjian, Honoré des Près, Susan Tabak, Parfumerie Générale, and Phaedon.

LUXURIOUS VINTAGE CLOTHES

So many fabulous, private, haute couture wardrobes, so few open doors. Paris is the city of secret upscale garment collections. "Vintage" here is less a commercial business than a family matter. Nathalie Dufour, director of Andam (the official fashion award of the French Ministry of Culture), regularly roams her neighborhood (Palais Royal) for secondhand-clothes shops. She will dig up fabulous designer wares that she alters or customizes, as do the smart ladies of Paris. Here a few of her favorite haunts in the city.

ANOUSCHKA ARCHIVE & PATRIMOINE

6, avenue du Coq, 75009
Tel. +33 1 48 74 37 00
E-mail: contact@anouschka.fr

Ask any fashion fiend in Paris and they'll all utter the same words: "a cavern of Ali Baba." Anouschka is a Parisian character, former model, queen of the night, traveler, costume designer for films . . . She started collecting clothes in the 1980s, and over the last twenty-five years she has handpicked a world-class selection of treasures, from the 1920s to the Montana era, in mint condition. Her work of love and dedication is showcased in a 3,230-square-foot apartment (she fills three other warehouses), by appointment only. Major stylists and designers from all over the world make a pilgrimage here whenever they're in Paris, for consulting, collaboration, rental, or a friendly hi. Bonus: Her staff is equally passionate and knowledgeable.

DIDIER LUDOT

20, 24, galerie de Montpensier, 75001
Tel. +33 1 42 96 06 56

LA PETITE ROBE NOIRE

125, galerie de Valois, 75001
Tel. +33 1 40 15 01 04

The first store is dedicated to vintage haute couture clothes, the second to couture accessories, the third to LBDs. Inside the Jardins du Palais Royal, the three consignment stores are all eminent and internationally acclaimed, including by the most famous Hollywood celebrities' stylists.

GABRIELLE GEPPERT

31 & 34, galerie de Montpensier, 75001

Tel. +33 1 42 61 53 52

This neighbor of **DIDIER LUDOT** (see p. 150) always catches Dufour's attention with "good Chanel bags, affordable reptile pouches, plenty of 1980s treasures, and also the YSL trench in black vinyl of *Belle du jour.*"

RAGTIME

23, rue de l'Échaudé, 75006

Tel. +33 1 56 24 00 36

On Rive Gauche, the store of revered Françoise Auguet is small, untidy, but fascinating. She is an authority on fashion history, her store—pricey, indeed—is the best place to find pristine Dior and 1930s silk gowns.

RAG

81, rue Saint-Honoré, 75001

Tel. +33 1 40 28 48 44

Fashion stylists love this selection of jaunty YSL Rive Gauche, Valentino Couture, and furs—lots of furs—courtesy of Manu, the curator, a fan of the 1980s who loves to divulge his best finds.

NEILA VINTAGE & DESIGN

28, rue du Mont-Thabor, 75001

Tel. +33 1 42 96 88 70

A museumlike store, beloved by the likes of Gaïa Repossi, with a well-curated, upscale selection. Hard to find anything if you're on a budget but definitely worth a visit, at least for inspiration.

VINTAGE CLOTHING PARIS

10, rue de Crussol, 75011

Tel. +33 1 48 07 16 40

In the Oberkampf area, not far from Le Cirque d'Hiver, treasures by Mugler, Hermès, and Alaïa, with an inventory spanning the 1930s to the '80s. Brigitte's store is, famously, seldom open (Wednesday to Saturday, 2:00 PM to 7:00 PM), but you can set up an appointment outside the shop's regular hours. A favorite of Yazbukey for vintage jewelry, as well.

LA JOLIE GARDE-ROBE

15, rue Commines, 75003

Tel. +33 1 42 72 13 90

Another Yazbukey haunt, this vintage shop is a gold mine for clothes and jewelry from the romantic 1920s to the disco 1980s. Come and pick anything Marie, the knowledgeable owner and curator of the place, suggests for you.

CHEZEL

59, rue Condorcet, 75009

Tel. +33 1 53 16 47 31

Often advertised as the cheap alternative to DIDIER LUDOT (p. 150), especially for YSL (a lot), Lanvin, and Céline. Plus, the boutique is well curated and well kept by the owners (mum and daughter), friendly, and easy to browse.

Mid-Range Secondhand

VINTAGE BAR (16, rue de la Verrerie, 75004; Tel. +33 1 42 74 56 95) caters to seekers of Louis Vuitton, Paco Rabanne, Chanel, Dior, and Hermès accessories. Mainly, it is a paradise for those who cling to furs, new and clean at bargain prices. AÏSSA & CO (formerly SINCE, 32, rue Saint Roch, 75001; Tel. +33 1 49 27 93 11) offers contemporary vintage by high-end specialists, with racks full of Gaultier, YSL, and Alaïa. BDA (46, rue de la Condamine, 75017; Tel. +33 1 42 93 54 70), Bastien De Almeida's "glam-o-rama" store, deals in Las Vegas and Hollywood gowns from the 1930s to 1980s. With a specialized bookstore (nightlife culture and musicals) and couture workshops. MAMIE (73 rue de Rochechouart, 75009; Tel. +33 1 42 82 09 98): There are two stores side by side in this area of Pigalle, but the one you want to visit is the pink one with real clothes and accessories from the 1900s to the 1980s for men, women, and children. At THANX GOD I'M A VIP (12, rue de Lancry, 75010; Tel. +33 1 42 03 02 09), Sylvie Chateigner, former queen of the night, offers two floors: Givenchy, Prada, and Lanvin, plus cheaper trades downstairs. By the Canal Saint-Martin, visit CHEZ PAULETTE (32, rue Bichat, 75010; Tel. +33 1 42 08 92 76), a lovely shop with immaculate 1960s, '70s, and '80s items. Lots of colors, with cool accessories from Cardin, Gucci, and Torrente. For two floors of secondhand wares, stop by COME ON EILEEN (16, rue des Taillandiers, 75011; Tel. +33 1 43 38 12 11), with some nice surprises (Cardin, YSL . . .), plus tons of dandy clothes and some real vintage (Courrèges). Also, great jewelry. MODE DE VUE (53 rue de Turenne, 75003; Tel. +33 1 42 77 02 88) carries vintage and contemporary designer sunglasses from the 1950s to now.

CONSIGNMENT STORES

Recycle your last-season upscale castoff here. They will be in good hands for a second chance.

RÉCIPROQUE
89, 92, 93, 95, 97, 101, rue de la Pompe, 75016
Tel. +33 1 47 04 30 28

With six boutiques, this consignment-store empire, self-proclaimed the largest in Paris, is the most open secret among the stealth-wealth world of the 16th arrondissement. Gowns, hats, cocktail dresses, furs, bags. The plus is the organization by designer.

WK ACCESSORIES
5, rue du Marché-Saint-Honoré, 75001
Tel. +33 1 40 20 99 76

Anytime the fashion belles feel like adding a good bag to their collection, this is the place they head for. Tiny but smart.

ÉCRIN DE MODE
6, rue de Jarente, 75004
Tel. +33 9 81 82 00 66

Sarah Canonica, ex–marketing executive, used to work at Erès and Céline. Her consignment store is definitely on the map for coveted secondhand, last-season treasures, and even prototypes: Chanel, Lanvin, YSL, Lacroix, Kenzo, Dior, even sometimes Patou and Emanuelle Khanh. Also a good source for high-end bags and shoes.

CHEAP AND FUN

In the mood for fun? Short on cash? Head for a hunt in a *friperie*—cheap, messy heaps of used frocks, shoes, and stuff, regarded as inspiration by high-end designers and as commodities by fashion students. If you know the art of leisurely hunting in uncharted territories and don't mind the subsequent hours of alterations and repairs on your torn picks, then you'll really enjoy the air of *Desperately Seeking Susan* these places provide.

KILLIWATCH
64, rue Tiquetonne, 75002
Tel. +33 1 42 21 17 37

The mecca of trendy secondhand addresses but deemed too expensive by our fashion interns since it started selling collections of edgy streetwear as well.

HIPPY MARKET

3, rue de Turbigo, 75001

Tel. +33 1 44 88 27 82

The Killiwatch spin-off: more affordable, easy to browse, and well organized. Your best bet for 1970s long skirts, flowery dresses, teddy blousons, small leather bags, and colorful cardigans.

EPISODE

12–16, rue Tiquetonne, 75002

Tel. +33 1 42 61 14 65

This Netherlands-originated secondhand chain is a hit, thanks to its daily intake, which is clearly organized: 25 € prom/party dresses, macramé skirts, boots, bags.

FREE'P'STAR

8, rue Sainte-Croix-de-la-Bretonnerie, 75004

Tel. +33 1 42 77 63 43

61, rue de la Verrerie, 75004

Tel. +33 1 42 78 00 76

20, rue de Rivoli, 75004

Tel. +33 1 42 77 63 43

Crammed and touristy to the point that you might feel queasy and try to leave immediately in search of better-curated spots. But if you like playing the hit-or-miss game, you can spend hours here, including heading down to the basement for the leather-jackets section. From there, you can continue rummaging endlessly through the Marais: no less than twenty fripperies to visit!

GUERRISOL

96, boulevard de Barbès, 75018
Tel. +33 1 53 28 10 70
Other locations: guerrisol.com

Legendary addresses in a very popular district of town, famous
for their piles and racks of low-low-low-end prices: 10€ stilettos
and wool coats; 1€ button-downs and tie-dye; battered, sequined
1980s dresses and men's suits . . . Not for the faint of heart or the
too-well-heeled, but it's where you'll dig out some 2011 Versace
for H&M.

FLEA MARKETS

One of the most touristic-fun things to do in Paris. Don't really
expect to score bargains, but definitely a nice, uplifting walk.

MARCHÉ AUX PUCES DE SAINT-OUEN

Porte de Clignancourt, 75018

Here's how to stroll this famous outdoor flea market with Anouschka,
our vintage pundit: Avoid the gaudy "clothes" part and browse
the antiques booths, where you can find loads of *merveilles*. At
MARCHÉ VERNAISON, check near the entrance for the booth
specializing in beads, glitter, sequins, and buttons. Then head to
Mme Giovanonni's booth 141, at the corner of alleys 7 and 3:
"Treasures of blouses, lace, but also sheets, towels, and lots of
curiosities," promises Anouschka. DAVID ROY (booth 3, aisle 1,
99 rue des Rosiers, 93400 Saint-Ouen), is the largest flea and quite
pricey but displays Chanel handbags and suits galore. Same with
CHRISTINE L (booth 84, aisle 5, 99 rue des Rosiers, 93400
Saint-Ouen), full of very expensive couture bags and jewelry.

Farther up, at MARCHÉ SERPETTE, Anouschka recommends VOYAGES, Elisio and Francis's stand (booth 10, alley 3), for all the Hermès bags, from purses to suitcases. CLARA LARDE (booth 28, aisle 1, 110 rue de Rosiers) is also a good source for tasteful vintage buys. NICOLAS, alley 6, is the top specialist for art and curiosities. Check also LE MONDE DU VOYAGE (booth 15, aisle 3, 110 rue de Rosiers, 93400 Saint-Ouen) for luggage (Vuitton, Hermès). End your tour at GALERIE JAMES (booths 17–19, alley 4; see p. 163).

At MARCHÉ PAUL BERT, PASCAL JUSTE's stand (booth 40, alley 2) is a must-stop for jewelry, furniture, decorative tables, precious boxes, mirrors: "Anything to design yourself a fabulous walk-in closet." For design, Anouschka always stops at Xavier Missakian's VINYLRECORDS & DESIGN (booth 73 bis, alley 1) for his '70s collectors, and to RAPHAEL DRUET (booth 136, alley 1) for Scandinavian design. (NB: MARCHÉ PAUL BERT is a also great stop for people-watching and comfort food.)

At MARCHÉ DAUPHINE, visit FALBALAS (booths 284 and 285, 1st floor, 140, rue des Rosiers, 94300 Saint-Ouen; Tel. +33 6 10 58 58 78; falbalas.puces.free.fr for directions). Among the best dealers of authentic vintage items in Paris. The selection of clothes covers the eighteenth century to the late 1970s.

PUCES DE VANVES
Avenue de la Porte de Vanves /rue Marc Sangnier, 75014

Caveat: Get there before 8:00 AM, and don't expect as much fashion as antiques, decorations, and tchotchkes. Tasteful, with great finds in rare books, as well. A favorite of stylish American visitors. Saturdays and Sundays only.

DECORATION

AD France is our reference magazine and compass for design addresses and decoration tips. The journalists always know where to find the glitz that appeals to decoration specialists but also fashion people. Below, a short "best-of" by expert Sophie Pinet.

GALERIE KREO
31, rue Dauphine, 75006
Tel. +33 1 53 10 23 00

The not-to-be-missed kingdom of international design in Paris. All the stars are here, from Marc Newson to Bouroullec, and high-end patrons, from Lapo Elkan to great design pundit Karl Lagerfeld, who swears by "their eye" and "their artistic discoveries." The gallery sees itself as a research laboratory, producing, curating, and exhibiting museum-level creations and limited editions.

JOUSSE ENTREPRISE
18, rue de Seine, 75006
Tel. +33 1 53 82 13 60
Also, a contemporary gallery:
6, rue Saint-Claude, 75003
Tel. +33 1 53 82 10 18

The gallery is a renowned platform for the best vintage classics, like Jean Prouvé, Charlotte Perriand, Jean Royère, Le Corbusier, etc. It is also the Paris dealer of the fashion legend Rick Owens, also known for his "gothic minimal" furniture in glass fiber, resin, cashmere, and bone.

GALERIE PATRICK SEGUIN
5, rue des Taillandiers, 75001
Tel. +33 1 47 00 32 35

One of the most important addresses for vintage design in Paris, one that regularly breaks records in international sales and fairs like Design Miami. It's rumored that Vladimir Doronin—Naomi Campbell's boyfriend—stops here when he yearns for a six-figure polar bear sofa.

GALERIE DOWNTOWN FRANÇOIS LAFFANOUR
18 & 33, rue de Seine, 75006
Tel. +33 1 46 33 82 41 and +33 1 53 10 32 32

"Unmissable" for the fans of Jean Prouvé, this gallery specializes in twentieth-century vintage furniture made in Europe and America. A diehard fan is Isabel Marant: "The owner, François Laffanour, has been collecting furniture from my favorite designers for the past twenty-eight years. I love to swing by his *galerie* to contemplate some amazing pieces: an armchair by Prouvé, lamps by Serge

Mouille, intelligent bookshelves by Perriand . . . All those great, timeless furniture pieces with sleek lines I love so much."

GUILLAUME

3, rue Sainte-Anastase, 75003

Tel. +33 1 57 40 61 43

A small address opened by a real character, with a stunning selection of pieces mostly from the 1970s: brass furniture, vintage *Facade* magazines, enameled boxes from Loulou de la Falaise's estate, Madeleine Castaing's ashtrays. The perfect place for the perfect gift.

INDIA MAHDAVI

19, rue Las Cases, 75007

Tel. +33 1 45 55 88 88

Furniture to die for, and recently another store dedicated to small objects. This designer and architect embodies the *bobo* lifestyle of the Left Bank, as displayed in the trendy HÔTEL THOUMIEUX (see p. 76). The international jet set loves the colorful and neo-retro aesthetic.

MAISON DARRÉ

32, rue du Mont-Thabor, 75001

Tel. +33 1 42 60 27 97

A surrealist world that perfectly matches the one designer Yazbukey celebrates in her fall 2013 collection, driving the too-cool-for-school international posse to the tiny gallery. The dandy Vincent Darré— also designer of Le Baron in NYC—always launches his own collections with whimsical cocktail parties held here during Fashion Weeks.

GALERIE JAMES
Serpette, allée 4, booths 17–19, Marché aux Puces Saint-Ouen

Paul Viguier is not even thirty, not only model good-looking but also and already the promising name of the Saint-Ouen flea market. He specializes in Brazilian modernism from the 1950s to the '70s, with names that get the connoisseurs such as Joaquim Tenreiro and Sergio Rodriguez, excited.

GALERIE NEXTLEVEL
8, rue Charlot, 75003
Tel. +33 1 44 54 90 88

The international scene of fledgling designers is nestled in this gallery of the upper Marais, created and managed by Isabelle Mesnil. She fosters designers flirting with art and also curates regular original-photo exhibitions.

GALERIE BSL
23, rue Charlot, 75003
Tel. +33 1 44 78 94 14

Another hip gallery of the Marais, getting its cool reputation with its contemporary design, twentieth-century lights, and also a great roster of tasteful artists' jewelry (including Ron Arad).

RUE HÉROLD
8, rue Herold, 75001
Tel. +33 1 42 33 66 56

"It's Margiela meets Comme des Garçons on the fabrics field," sums up an enthusiastic friend. Charlotte de la Grandière, the owner and stylist, sells incredible fabrics she finds in Japan, France, and Italy by the yard. Very selective. Some fashion customers bring these decoration fabrics to their bespoke tailors.

LINDELL & CO.

14, rue du Grand-Prieuré, 75011

Tel. +33 1 43 57 43 42

Gabrielle Soyer is a Scandinavian textile designer. She launched her own home-furnishings house in Paris in 2008. The address where all the Parisian decorators flock for Asian splendor, including the most beautiful pillows in the world, woven or hand embroidered in India. Also rugs, sheets, and fabrics by the yard.

ASTIER DE VILLATTE

173, rue Saint-Honoré, 75001

Tel. +33 1 42 60 74 13

"Very Frenchy, a bit cheesy, but always endearing," says a friend. Created fifteen years ago by Benoît Astier de Villatte and Ivan Pericoli, this house boasts a unique hand-production of vintage-looking ceramic—recently, a collaboration with John Derian—old press-printed agendas, beauty products, antique furniture, silverware, etc. Plan B: For gifts, consider a visit to CIRE TRUDON (78, rue de la Seine, 75006; Tel. +33 1 43 26 46 50). Its genealogy boasts origins back to the Manufacture Royale des cires (royal candlemakers), but it also shows a great love for new creators.

GALERIE MAY

23, rue de Lille, 75007

Tel. +33 1 42 61 41 40

The artist Maylis Queyrat was born in the 1970s, the decade she is selling most in her new gallery of contemporary decorative arts, another trendy address in Paris. She wants to reinvent the "neo-bourgeois" aesthetic with her editions of preciously crafted furniture.

GALERIE CHAHAN

11, rue de Lille, 75007

Tel. +33 1 47 03 47 00

This antiques and interior-design dealer is a big hit of the Carré Rive Gauche, the well-bred area of *antiquaires*. As popular in Paris as in LA and Miami, Chahan Minassian is your go-to gallery for US furniture from the 1930s to the '60s.

GALERIE VAN DER STRAETEN

11, rue Ferdinand-Duval, 75004

Tel. +33 1 42 78 99 99

Hervé Van Der Straeten is not only a gifted designer but also a real fashion insider (partner of the shoe designer Bruno Frisoni). He still sells his architectural necklaces and earrings on Net-à-porter. His main activity, though, centers on his collection of exclusive furniture and lighting, neo-baroque, radical, and elegant, exhibited in his own gallery alongside the work of guest artists.

GALERIE DESIGN & ANTIQUAIRE ERIC PHILIPPE

25, galerie Vero-Dodat, 75001

Tel. +33 1 42 33 28 26

Extremely chic, in the gorgeous nineteenth-century passage where Louboutin can also be found, behind the Palais Royal. Rick Owens and Karl Lagerfeld are rumored to be fans of his furniture and objects from the Scandinavian school (1920–60) as well as Nordic and American designers from the fifties.

CARPENTERS WORKSHOP GALLERY
54, rue de la Verrerie, 75004
Tel. +33 1 42 78 80 92

Established by a duo of ambitious entrepreneurs, this gallery shows
limited-edition pieces of established designers (Atelier Van Lieshout,
Maarten Baas . . .). They sell madly all over the world (two other
galleries in London), supposedly including to hip-hop honchos
like P Diddy.

GALERIE RÉFRACTAIRE

26, boulevard Saint-Germain, 75005

Tel. +33 1 43 54 39 90

The exclusive gallery of aesthete François Dorléans looks like a retro apartment or a cabinet of curiosities more than a store. The owner lives here, but everything is for sale. Perfect for finding exotic and original objects, such as lightweight, Onouh coral, eighteenth-century Venetian chairs. By appointment, or from Tuesday to Saturday, 2:30 PM to 7:30 PM.

DEYROLLE

46, rue du Bac, 75007

Tel. +33 1 42 22 32 21

Since 1831, this landmark has been the most impressive cabinet of curiosities and taxidermy collections in Europe, highlighted by Woody Allen in *Midnight in Paris*. Entirely reconstructed after an arson incident in 2008, it is still the favorite of many stylists, like Viktor & Rolf, for its endless possibilities of surrealist dreams.

BROCANTE BAROQUE PARISIENNE

22, avenue de la Porte de Saint-Ouen, 75018

Tel. +33 1 46 27 73 36

Original design and art, pop retro, from the 1950s to the 1970s (Steiner sofas, Ingo Maurer lamps . . .), selected for fifteen years by the friendly Jean-Pierre Kanizsay. An address approved by fashion designer Vanessa Seward.

MIGHT BE
USEFUL
ONE DAY

FLOWERS

In Paris, you don't just send beautiful flowers. You send beautiful flowers from the right place.

LACHAUME
103, rue Faubourg Saint-Honoré, 75008
Tel. +33 1 42 60 59 74

Maître fleuriste since 1845, this respectable house is a favorite of Karl Lagerfeld. It has recently moved from its historic boutique on rue Royale, but the tradition of grandiosity—rooted in a Venetian savoir-faire—remains constant . . . "Since the lovely Caroline and her sister manage the shop after their grandmother, the flowers are even more beautiful," states the emperor of good taste.

STÉPHANE CHAPELLE
29, rue de Richelieu, 75001
Tel. +33 1 42 60 65 66

A specialist in stage sets and floral accessories inspired by haute couture and produced in his elegant Palais Royal workshop. The go-to horticultural wizard for many fashion houses, who tout his dramatic sense of design.

BAPTISTE FLEURS
At Hermès
17, rue de Sèvres, 75006
Tel. +33 1 42 84 19 08

Rare flowers wrapped in the orange paper of the luxury house in the stunning setting of the 1935 Lutétia Hotel swimming pool, revamped by Hermès.

ODORANTES

9, rue Madame, 75006

Tel. +33 1 42 84 03 00

A firsthand address for gorgeous vintage roses like the famous Black Baccara. Emmanuel Sammartino, a former makeup artist, has reportedly been handling—with his partner, Christophe Hervé— bouquets for the likes of Sofia Coppola for more than eight years.

MOULIÉ FLEURS

8, place Palais-Bourbon, 75007

Tel. +33 1 45 51 78 43

A short leap from the offices of international Condé Nast, the National Assembly, and Rick Owens's mansion (the former office of President François Mitterand), this old-timer specializes in prestigious floral arrangements for spectacular events. So fashion-forward that Estée Lauder gave its name to a rose nail polish in its fall 2012 collection.

L'ARTISAN FLEURISTE

95, rue Vieille-du-Temple, 75003
Tel. +33 1 42 78 40 40

A high-spirited team for custom-made bouquets of all sorts and sizes (gorgeous tulips and peonies). Patronized by fashion brands like Alexander McQueen and Kris Van Assche.

ATELIER VERTUMNE

12, rue de La Sourdière, 75001
Tel. +33 1 42 86 06 76

Clarisse Béraud, the flower artist, is regarded as one of the most gifted and trendy in Paris. She is a favorite of Christophe Robin, the prince of hair artists, and can claim references from major fashion houses.

LE JARDIN D'ANTOINE

57, rue de la Pompe, 75016
Tel. +33 1 45 04 29 39

Antoine Teixeira is a discrete artisan but renowned for bold, sculptural, dramatic arrangements, with the most exceptional examples of rare and timely flowers ever.

FABRICS AND SEWING

Best places for amateurs or professionals to source their devices, raw materials, and best inspiration.

MARCHÉ SAINT-PIERRE

2, rue Charles Nodier, 75018
Tel. +33 1 46 06 92 25

A Zola kind of store, right up the Montmartre Butte, where any Parisian girl will head at some point or another during her year. Six floors of decoration and ready-to-wear fabrics and sewing materials. Hasn't changed much since its opening more than sixty years ago. Cheap, crowded, fun . . . For basics only.

MOKUBA

18, rue de Montmartre, 75001
Tel. +33 1 40 13 02 26

More and more ribbons in silk, satin, lace, leather, and metallic. A spectacular showroom, famous among the couture houses of Paris.

ULTRAMOD

4, rue de Choiseul, 75002
Tel. +33 1 42 96 98 30

Since the 1920s, a must for anyone who likes to customize garments, with very affordable prices and an endearing ambiance of *autrefois*. All you ever want to know about buttons, ribbons, and trimmings.

FASHION ARCHIVES / BOOKSTORES

The major international bookstores for fashion and decoration ideas in Paris are well known. GALIGNANI (224, rue de Rivoli, 75001; Tel. +33 1 42 60 76 07), the leader for two hundred years, is a bottomless cavern of decorative art and fashion catalogs. For a splurge on the latest issues of international magazines, head to WHSMITH (248, rue de Rivoli 75001; Tel. +33 1 44 77 88 99). BRENTANO'S (37, avenue de l'Opéra, 75002; Tel. +33 1 42 60 87 37), the third of these English-speaking bookstores in Paris dealing in coffee-table books and fashion inspiration, is not as much visited as LA HUNE (16, rue de l'Abbaye, 75006; Tel. +33 1 45 48 35 85), another Isabel Marant haunt ("open superlate at night, perfect for my hunts for architecture books!"). Designers and their assistants also harvest heaps of catalogs at the BOOKSTORE OF MUSÉE DES ARTS DÉCORATIFS (107, rue de Rivoli, 75001; Tel. +33 1 42 60 64 95). Here are the other best places for fashion-image addicts. Fans converge on these stores on pilgrimages from all over the world.

7L
7, rue de Lille, 75007
Tel. +33 1 42 92 03 58

Karl Lagerfeld, the biggest bookworm in fashion, opened his own bookstore in the heart of the Carré Rive Gauche in December 1999. A sumptuous space dedicated to beautiful books, where the maître also hides his photo studio. Among other treasures, everything by his friend and sometimes copublisher Steidl. His advice: "I especially like three booksellers: Hervé, Catherine, and Vincent."

OFR

20, rue Dupetit-Thouars, 75003

Tel. +33 1 42 45 72 88

Alexandre and Marie Thumerelle have moved their international magazines (edgy and unmissable) into the villagelike Carreau du Temple area, not far from the newspaper *Liberation*'s HQ. Everything, from all over the world: magazines, fanzines, and books on the recent and worthy in photography, art, architecture, design, fashion, decoration . . .

COMPTOIR DE L'IMAGE

44, rue de Sévigné, 75003

Tel. +33 1 42 72 03 92

A cult location for any stylist. Ramshackle-looking, crammed with rare photography books, old-fashioned look books, and vintage magazines from the 1990s, like the brilliant UK *The Face*, Matthias Vriens's *Dutch*, or the first *Purple* magazine.

LES ARCHIVES DE LA PRESSE

51, rue des Archives, 75003

Tel. +33 1 42 72 63 93

Weeklies and monthlies from the nineteenth century to now, including a nice section for fashion (old *Le Petit Echo de la Mode* or *Elle* from the postwar era), lifestyle and historic political news magazines like *Paris Match*, as well as department-store and luxury-brand catalogs.

LIBRAIRIE LA GALCANTE

52, rue de l'Arbre Sec, 75001

Tel. +33 1 44 77 87 44

E-mail: lagalcante@lagalcante.com

A boutique museum of old French newspapers and magazines, including fashion. Find old, sold-out issues of *Vogue*, *Elle*, *Harper's Bazaar*, but also cult French magazines from the 1980s, such as *Depeche Mode*, *Glamour*, and *Jardin des Modes*.

GALLIÉRA

At Musée de la mode de la ville de Paris

10, avenue Pierre Ier de Serbie, 75016

Tel. +33 1 56 52 86 00

Closed until fall 2013, but its fabulous archives are open by appointment to fashion professionals. For exhibitions, head to LES DOCKS — CITÉ DE LA MODE ET DU DESIGN (34, quai d'Austerlitz, 75013; Tel. +33 1 76 77 25 30).

SHOE REPAIR

Make these pros your best friends to keep your heels looking brand new.

GÉRARD PULIN

5, rue Chauveau-Lagarde, 75008

Tel. +33 1 42 65 08 57

A real cobbler, a specialist in women's shoes since 1946. Head here to get new soles in any color or material or to fix any upscale brand, from Pierre Hardy to Hermès. A French *Vogue* favorite for slightly trimming down their six-inch heels.

MINUIT MOINS 7
10, passage Véro-Dodat, 75001
Tel. +33 1 42 21 15 47

Like everyone else, get ready to fall in love. Opened near Louboutin in the romantic passage Véro-Dodat, this is the trendiest shoe repair shop in town. This artisan masters everything about red soles, high-heel reduction, and couture-shoe woes. Pricey, indeed, but soooo sexy.

L'ATELIER D'ANTOINE
75, rue de Miromesnil, 75008
Tel. +33 1 42 93 21 29

This rock 'n' roll-looking shoe repairer can do anything, on the most sophisticated stilettos or boots.

NESSIM ATTAL
122, rue d'Assas, 75006
Tel. +33 1 46 34 52 33

Another expert at his craft, indeed. You can bring him a drawing of your dream gladiators, and he'll make it come true.

DOMINIQUE BARILERO
5, rue Amélie, 75007
Tel. +33 1 45 51 29 53

He learned his craft with John Lobb, and he's reputed to work seated in an old-fashioned, cross-legged position or on his knees.

ATELIER CATTELAN

2, rue Melingue, 75019

Tel. +33 1 42 08 58 18

128, rue de Grenelle, 75007

Tel. +33 1 45 55 17 70

Even if the Saint-Germain-des-Prés location seems more convenient, the real fashion connoisseurs trek to the original store, Buttes Chaumont, for the trickiest work on their Christian Dior heels or for a new color (*patine*).

VANEAU

44, rue Vaneau, 75007

Tel. +33 1 42 22 06 94

45, rue Vivienne, 75002

Tel. +33 1 45 08 1798

And three other addresses

Yves Saint Laurent left a signed photo from the time he used to live on rue de Babylone. This classy shoe repairer is still a relevant address for any couturelike item.

CLARASO

136, rue Montmatre, 75002

Tel. +33 1 42 36 14 45

82, rue du Bac, 75007

Tel. +33 1 45 49 46 37

And five other addresses

An institution, still popular, still handy, even if its popularity seems to have worn out a bit because of its lackluster service. For basic repairs on expensive shoes.

DRY CLEANING

Because you can't take the risk of someone scratching that silk-satin Lanvin dress of yours.

PRESSING DE LA MADELEINE

12, rue Arcade, 75008

Tel. +33 1 42 65 30 11

A friend swears that they erase even dirty bicycle-oil stains on a Burberry trench. They can also repair minor tears in your favorite Sonia Rykiel knits and give you the best tips on fixing anything yourself.

TEINTURERIE DE L'ÉTOILE

20, rue Jean Giraudoux, 75016

Tel. +33 1 47 20 74 36

The Harry Winston of dry cleaning. One of the rare places in Paris where Chanel would send haute couture and precious embroideries. The owner used to be legendary Mme Benaim. She left in 2010, but the overqualified staff remains.

PRESSING DU LOUVRE

4, rue Bailleul, 75001

Tel. +33 1 42 60 31 87

A famous name for major houses of haute couture, this dry cleaner is the only one recommended in Paris for contemporary fabrics— say, silk layered with *caoutchouc*.

TEINTURERIE DELAPORTE

62, rue François 1er, 75008

Tel. +33 1 43 59 82 11

An institution since 1905. Still okay for *nettoyages* on any fabric "from today or yesterday," as their website claims. Can also come to the home, work on hats or "wedding dresses with 2,000 fine pearls."

TEINTURERIE GERMAINE

11, bis rue de Surène, 75008

Tel. +33 1 42 65 12 28

TEINTURERIE STAR, CENTRE COMMERCIAL ITALIE 2

30, avenue d'Italie, 75013

Tel. +33 1 45 80 17 06

With DELAPORTE (above), the two other addresses of the same family, boasting a certificate of excellence "awarded to my mother-in-law by the French President Auriol in 1943," explains the high-quality heiress, Madame Joelle of Italie 2 (she will recognize you five years later after one visit. Hence, nothing ever gets lost). Specializing in waterproofing, suede, and leather at great prices, but also any tricky stains on couture or wedding dresses.

ALTERATIONS

Bring your vintage troves and make them look as if they've been yours forever.

STYL'UP
5, rue Pasquier, 75008
Tel. +33 1 42 66 44 85
A perfect tailor trusted by the most fashionable ladies, including the A-class stylists and international socialites who bring their vintage couture treasures here to have them resized for a perfect fit.

DIAMANT COUTURE

15, rue Molière, 75001

Tel. +33 1 42 60 99 61

Can fix anything—the reason Acne would send you here when you need to adjust a waist or a hem. A specialist also in leather and fur. Plan B: in the same area, LI COUTURE (3, rue Thérèse, 75001; Tel. +33 1 42 44 13 33).

CECI EST UN TAILLEUR

65, rue de Turenne, 75003

Tel. +33 1 48 87 05 85

A recommendation from L'ÉCLAIREUR (see p. 137), this tailor can also work on bespoke men's suits or shirts. Open on Sundays, closed on Saturdays.

ÉLYSÉES 34

34, ave des Champs-Élysées, 75008

Tel. +33 1 42 89 65 99

Another tailor recommended by the retail experts of L'ÉCLAIREUR (see p. 137). They can work on menswear or womenswear and are also a trusted address for leather. Very reasonably priced—a special surprise in this prestigious neighborhood—inside a famous Champs-Élysées gallery.

AIT HAMADOUCHE HAMID

9, rue Saint-Sulpice, 75006

Tel +33 1 53 10 83 03

A great professional—where all the buttonhole maniacs converge when they want perfect, timely work at a reasonable price.

BENJAMIN

9, place de la Madeleine, 75009 (inside the Gallery)
Tel. +33 1 40 17 00 51

A real tailor with a beautiful work ethic, used to the best designer clothes and the most subtle work *à l'ancienne*.

ZELDA COUTURE

1, rue des Fossés-Saint-Jacques, 75005
Tel. +33 1 44 41 08 68

The specialist in denim repair in Paris, an address provided by the Diesel stores. The owner, a real pundit on any jeans-related issue, has closed his convenient outpost in the Sentier but is still personally available in his 5th-arrondissement studio, by the Jardin du Luxembourg.

CREDITS

ILLUSTRATIONS
Caroline Andrieu—untitled-07.com

COVER
Calla Haynes

ILLUSTRATION CREDITS
Céline Spring-Summer 2013, p. 2; Carven Spring-Summer 2013
at Le Bon Marché Rive-Gauche, p. 10; Café de Flore, p. 12;
Le Floréal, p. 28; Palais-Royal, p. 40; Viktor and bag Yazbukey
Spring-Summer 2013, p. 49; Aurélie Bidermann Spring-Summer
2013, p. 53; Chez Jeannette, p. 56; Olympia Le-Tan Spring-Summer
2013, p.62; Crazy Horse, p. 66; Le Bristol, p. 71; Hôtel Thoumieux,
p. 76; David Mallett Salon, p. 82; Dior Institute at Plaza Athénée,
p. 102; Thai Home Spa, p. 108; Yazbukey jewelry, p. 115; Julien
David Spring-Summer 2013, p. 131; Balmain Spring-Summer 2013,
p.134; Alexander McQueen Spring-Summer 2013, p. 143; Ring Brise
Paille by Violaine Febvret, Gallery Naïla de Monbrison, p. 146;
Rick Owens furniture, p. 160; Deyrolle p. 166 ; Minuit Moins Sept
Shoe Repair, p. 168; Odorantes, p. 171; Karl Lagerfeld at his 7L
Bookstore, p. 174.

ACKNOWLEDGMENTS

A HUGE THANK-YOU TO:

Karl Lagerfeld
Loïc Prigent
Isabel Marant
Sarah—colette
Nathalie Dufour—Andam
Frédérique Verley—French *Vogue*
Viktor & Rolf
Anthony Vaccarello
Christopher Niquet
Yazbukey
Yasmine Eslami
Anouschka
Aurélie Bidermann
Virginie Mouzat—French *Vanity Fair*
Guillaume Henry—Carven
ACNE Studios & ACNE Paper
Lucien Pagès
Sébastien Peigné—Mugler
Sophie Pinet—*AD France*; theshapeofthejourney.com
Mimi Xu a.k.a. Misty Rabbit—soundcloud.com/mistyrabbit
Monica Feudi and Carola Guaineri—feudiguaineri.com

SPECIAL THANK-YOU TO:

Todd Selby—theselby.com
Deborah Aaronson—Abrams
Lisa Gallagher—Sanford. J. Greenburger Associates

THANK YOU FOR YOUR SUPPORT:

Sylvie Yeu, Laure Heriard Dubreuil, Celine and Delphine Danhier, Alexa Rodulfo, Lydie Diakhaté, Alais Diop, Cristina Ricupero, Karen de Loisy, Leila Chouaib, Géraldine Postel, Joe Hall, Muriel Mucha, Gillian Conroy, Françoise Portal, Bertrand Bordenave, Christina Schuhbeck, Maria Garozi, Beth Steidle, and Erin Curler and Raffe Jefferson at McNally Jackson Bookstore